*Carol*

# UNSEEN ODDS

# UNSEEN ODDS

## SPIRITUAL HAPPENINGS, GHOSTLY TALES, AND SPOOKY PRANKS FROM THE OLDEN DAYS

BY
SHIRLEY BAHLMANN

BONNEVILLE BOOKS ™
Springville, Utah

ISBN: 1-55517-734-4
e.1

Published by Bonneville Books
Imprint of Cedar Fort Inc.
www.cedarfort.com

Distributed by:

Cover design by Nicole Cunningham
Cover design © 2004 by Lyle Mortimer
Cover photo by Bob Bahlmann


Printed in the United States of America
10 9 8 7 6 5 4 3 2 1

Printed on acid-free paper

Library of Congress Cataloging-in-Publication Data

Bahlmann, Shirley.
  Unseen odds : spiritual happenings, ghostly tales, and spooky pranks from the olden days / by Shirley Bahlmann.
        p. cm.
  ISBN 1-55517-734-4 (pbk. : alk. paper)
1.  Ghost stories, American. 2.  Utah--Fiction.  I. Title.

PS3602.A44U57 2004
813'.0873308--dc22

                    2003020370

## DEDICATION

*For my sister Beverly, who recognized Grandpa Oscar Dean Anderson's photograph when she was a child, even though he died before she was born.*

# ACKNOWLEDGMENTS

I thank my lucky stars for my proofreaders Greg Anderson, Judi Hansen, Judy Gubler, Lannette Nielson, Linda Pratt, Val Sorensen, Larry and Gayelene Henrikson, Robert, Scott, and Heidi Bahlmann.

I also extend my thanks to Ilse Stringham for research help, and to Blair and Karen Likes for a promotional push! Thanks to Troy Osmond for contagious grin and his steadfast assistance.

A special thanks to Slick, the cat.

# TABLE OF CONTENTS

# FOREWORD

Are there really such things as ghosts? Are there spirits that possess some unseen power that allows them to interact with our ordinary lives and alter what we normally see and understand with our mortal minds?

Perhaps you can identify with Clyde Nielson's childhood memory of going to the graveyard at midnight to walk around the big headstone with the crying angel on top, her marble arms outstretched for a cold embrace. In the dark of night, he circled her three times before stopping and listening intently, heart pounding, muscles tensed for flight, only to hear the angel say nothing—nothing at all.

Maybe you are one who believes wholeheartedly in the elusive world of spirits. Perhaps you have even interacted with those from that unearthly realm. Some say that the spirit world is right here, all around us, yet most of us aren't tuned in to it.

Some say that there are no such things as ghosts.

I, myself, enjoy a good mystery and find ghost stories to be the ultimate "whodunit?" Researching and writing this book was a great adventure. Nearly every story in this collection was documented by the person it actually happened to, or someone who was there when it happened. Some were related by descendants of those who were brushed by spectral forces, and grew up hearing the haunting tales over and over again.

There are a couple of pranks within these pages, as well as tales of comfort, humor, miracles, unexplained events, some spirits who came to save, and some who came to scare. It is my hope that the diversity in this collection will satisfy everyone's fascination with the supernatural.

Now turn on all the lights, settle yourself in a chair in the corner where you have a good view of all the windows and doors so you won't have to crane your neck when you hear an unexpected noise, and prepare to brush shoulders with that eerie and tantalizing world of spirits.

# DISCLAIMER

The author has written these stories based on accounts that she read in historical documents or events she was told about. She has done her best to portray the information as accurately as possible, adding the creative details that give the story immediacy in the re-telling. She realizes that not everyone associated with the stories will necessarily agree on every particular detail, but she hopes that readers will enjoy these tales in the spirit in which they are written.

# ROCKING

I dashed inside the house, savoring the sudden warm aroma of roasting meat. Mama stood up from where she'd been feeding wood into the cook stove. "Adelaide! The floor!" she scolded me.

"Sorry, Mama," I said. I raised my skirt with one hand and walked carefully across the dirt floor to Mama. Sometimes it was hard to make my seven-year-old feet move slowly, but our family rule was that we never ran or skipped inside the house. This was strictly enforced, because if we disobeyed, the dust would get stirred up something awful, getting dirt into our food and making us girls sneeze.

Mama's cheeks bloomed pink from the heat of the stove, and strands of loose hair brushed her forehead. I held an envelope out to her, and she took it with a question on her face.

"Brother Ellis just brought it by," I explained. "He said to tell you sorry he didn't bring it sooner."

Mama turned the letter over. "It's from Willie," she exclaimed, tearing open the envelope and pulling out a single sheet of paper. Uncle Willie was Mama's younger brother who still lived in Spring City next to Granny. Mama unfolded the paper and began to read.

"No," Mama's voice came out choked and broken. "Mother," she mumbled. Mama stumbled backward and sat heavily in Granny's old rocking chair. I stood uncertainly by the stove, watching Mama rock and rock and rock, her hands over her face while her shoulders shook and tears dripped off her chin.

I shifted my feet uneasily. For as long as I could remember, the rocking chair had proudly claimed the only floor covering in the whole house. A braided rag rug cushioned the long, wooden rockers and kept them from working the floor into loose dirt. The chair beckoned to me at the end of a long day with the promise of a gentle ride, tipping me backward and forward,

1

backward and forward, in long, easy sweeps.

I loved that old rocking chair. Granny had given it to Mama when we'd moved away, over the mountain to Ferron. Sometimes Mama would sit and rock baby Eva to sleep, staring out the window at the eastern mountain range, and I knew she was thinking of Granny.

I remembered how Granny had cried when she found out that Papa was moving us away from Spring City. It was when we'd gone over to Granny's for the last time that she'd said, "Hannah, take the rocking chair."

"No, Mother," Mama protested. "You know how it soothes your aches and pains. I won't take it from you."

Granny took hold of both of Mama's hands and looked deep into her eyes. "You're not taking it. I'm giving it." Tears gathered in Granny's eyes. "I'd feel better knowing that you have it." Mama's chin quivered, then she and Granny hugged each other for a long time.

At first, moving to a broad flat of untamed land had been an adventure, but it soon lost its appeal. Papa built our cabin right in the middle of our homestead, which meant there were no neighbors to play with. I only had my sister Amanda who was two years older than me, and Elizabeth, who was three years younger. Eva came along after we'd moved, but there isn't much you can do with a baby except try to keep her from pulling your hair. I often wished we could live by Granny again. She was always glad to see me, even if I'd just been there the day before. She never mixed my name up with my sister's. Granny was a good cook too, whipping up the most delicious Swedish pancakes and little yellow butter cookies that could melt in your mouth. I know, because I ate one once without chewing it at all.

One Christmas, Granny sewed us girls matching dresses, the most beautiful blue with yellow flowers as bright as summer scattered across the fabric. I was delighted. I put mine on right away, twirling around to watch the skirt fan out until I was too dizzy to stand. Now I was wearing Amanda's dress because she had outgrown it, and Mama was saving mine for Elizabeth. I felt sorry that Amanda didn't have a Granny dress to wear anymore. When I wore the dress cut and sewn by my Granny's own two hands, I felt closer to her. Mama must have felt the same way about Granny's rocking chair.

The door burst open and Amanda came in, just back from town, holding four-year-old Elizabeth by the hand. "We're home!" Amanda called out. When she noticed Mama huddled in the rocking chair, she shot me a look of confusion. "What's the matter?" she asked softly. I shrugged my shoulders.

Elizabeth let go of Amanda and ran over to Mama. I didn't bother to remind her of the walking-in-the-house rule. "Mama," she cried, holding up her pudgy little arms. Mama scooped Elizabeth onto her lap and held her tightly as she kept on rocking.

Eva fussed in her cradle. Amanda walked over and picked her up, making shushing noises that sounded a lot like Mama's.

Papa paused in the doorway, taking in the scene with eyes buried under worried brows before he moved to Mama's side. "I passed Hyrum on the road," Papa said. "He told me he'd delivered a letter. What did it say, Hannah?"

Mama turned an anguished face up to Papa. "Mother died," she said just before a fresh wash of tears spilled down her face. She held the letter out for Papa to read. Papa took it from her trembling hand and read it silently.

"I'm so sorry, Hannah," he said, placing a gentle hand on her shoulder.

At his touch, Mama suddenly wiped her eyes with her sleeve and quickly set Elizabeth down on the floor. "I need to get ready," she said as she stood up.

"Ready for what?" Papa asked.

"The funeral," Mama said. She headed across the room to where her extra clothing hung on a hook by the bed.

"That's not a good idea."

Mama stopped suddenly, turned to stone by Papa's words. Ever so slowly, she twisted around to face Papa. "I have to go,

Edmund," she said, her eyes bright with old tears and fresh determination.

"Of course one of us must go," Papa said.

"One of us?" Mama repeated, her hands curling into fists at her sides.

Papa shrugged. "We can't just leave the farm and animals to take care of themselves."

"Someone from town can take care of the place while we're gone," Mama reasoned.

"That's not all," Papa said. "There are the girls." Eva began to whimper and squirm in Amanda's arms.

"We'll take them with us in the wagon," Mama said.

Papa shook his head. "There isn't time." He pointed to a line on the letter. "The funeral is tomorrow. There's no way we'd get the wagon through the canyon and over the mountain by then." Papa looked at us girls. "Besides, Eva's too young to travel."

Mama clenched her hands together in front of her skirt. "I have to go, Edmund." Her eyes pled with Papa.

"Hannah," Papa's voice came out soft. "I know you loved your mother. I'm as fond of your family as you are. They're like my own." Papa folded the letter and put it on the table. His voice was no-nonsense when he caught Mama's eyes and said, "Right now you're emotional. When you've had time to think it over, you'll see that the only thing that makes sense is for me to go for our whole family."

Mama stared at Papa for a long minute. She didn't seem to notice that Eva's fussing was turning into genuine cries of distress. Amanda bounced our little sister, trying to quiet her, but Eva only pushed at Amanda's chest with her little hands.

"She was my mother," Mama finally said to Papa, her quivering chin tipped up in defiance as she blinked her wet eyes.

"Yes," Papa said, his voice coming out agreeable but firm, "but you are needed here." He held his hand out toward the four of us girls standing in an uncertain little knot. Eva's eyes were filling with big tears of distress. Mama scanned our faces with quick, desperate eyes.

"There's got to be a way," she whispered miserably.

"The only way is for me to go," Papa answered, "and I've got to leave now if I'm going to make it."

Mama's back stiffened. "I want to go," she insisted.

Papa held his hands out, palms up. "There isn't time," he reasoned. "It isn't practical. I'm sorry your mother died, Hannah, but our own girls need their mama." As if to emphasize what Papa had said, Eva screamed out in frustration. Papa raised his voice to be heard over his youngest daughter. "Granny was a wonderful mother to you. You know she would want you to be the same for your own children."

Mama gave one little sob that caught in her throat before she clenched her jaw and whirled away from Papa. She stalked over to the stove and opened the door to reveal a sizzling venison roast. I had thought I wanted some, but now my stomach churned at the heavy aroma.

"Put some of that meat between a couple slices of bread so I can eat it along the road," Papa said. Mama didn't answer him, but pulled out the pan with a thick dishtowel wrapped around her hand and thumped it down on the stove top. She grabbed a knife and hacked a piece of meat free. She stalked over to the table and sawed two slices of bread from the loaf. She tossed the meat onto one slice and mashed the other one down on top of it.

"Thank you," Papa said as he scooped up the sandwich in one hand. "'Bye, girls," he called as he hurried out the door.

Mama took the squalling Eva out of Amanda's arms and sank down into the rocking chair. She kept her eyes averted from the window where she would have had a clear view of Papa riding for the canyon. Even though Eva was old enough to eat food with her eight little teeth, Mama began nursing her. The room became blessedly quiet. "Amanda," Mama said as dull as dust. "Please feed your sisters."

"Yes, Mama," Amanda answered. We ate in silence except for Elizabeth, who chattered on and on about her visit to town and seeing the horsies and other "widdle kids."

When Elizabeth stopped for a breath, I looked over at Mama. "Are you going to eat?" I asked.

"I'm not hungry," Mama said in a voice so small and sad that it scared me. I looked at Amanda, hoping that she would know what to do. She stared at Mama, then back at me, with eyes that mirrored the hopelessness in my heart. She didn't know what to do any more than I did.

We cleared up the dishes and put the food away without squabbling. When we were done, Mama stood up slowly from the chair. "Will you girls do the milking?" she asked in the same strange, flat voice.

"Yes," we answered together. Amanda and I looked at each other, delighted that we had spoken in unison. I took comfort from the coincidence.

After darkness settled over our lonely valley, Mama called us together for our nightly scripture reading. Then Mama offered a long prayer, punctuated with tears as she thanked Heavenly Father for Granny, and asked that Papa would be kept safe on his journey to the funeral. We all said "amen."

Amanda went with me and Elizabeth for a last trip to the outhouse before bed. When we got back inside, I was glad for the simple shelter of our small log house in the middle of the vast darkness outside.

While struggling to pull my nightgown over my head, the rocking chair took up its steady rhythm. I hoped Mama would soon find the comfort she needed to make her smile again. My head popped up through the neck hole and I glanced at the chair. It was rocking, all right, but Mama wasn't in it. No one was. My astonished eyes flew to Mama. She stopped changing Eva's diaper and slowly turned her wide eyes toward the chair that was rocking and rocking all by itself.

Amanda leaned in to Mama's side. "What's happening?" she asked in a whisper so low and frightened that I barely heard it over the noise of the rockers resolutely tipping back and forth, back and forth.

Mama pressed trembling fingers to her lips, her eyes

strangely alight. I took a step away from the chair that was busily rocking with no one in it.

Mama caught Eva up in her arms before she said softly, "It's Granny."

My heart fluttered at Mama's words, doubt tugging at my mind. "Isn't Granny dead?" I asked uncertainly, watching the empty chair as it tipped forward and back.

"Yes," Mama admitted. "Her spirit left her earthly body, but her spirit is still alive." Mama lowered herself slowly onto the edge of the bed, her eyes never leaving the chair, her face radiant. Eva reached her tiny arms toward the rocking chair, giggling with delight. Elizabeth snuggled in beside Mama's lap, giving the chair a shy smile.

Mama put her arm around my shoulders and drew me in closer. "We couldn't go to Granny's funeral, so she has came here to tell us goodbye." As soon as Mama spoke these words, the chair gradually slowed, then stopped. In the quiet that followed, a wash of warm love coursed through my body from the top of my head clear out through my fingers and toes. My eyes filled with unexpected tears. I glanced at Mama. She was crying, too, even though her smile was bright. Amanda was blinking back tears as she absently stroked Elizabeth's hair.

As soon as the chair stilled, Eva and Elizabeth turned their eyes away, no longer interested. Elizabeth looked up at Mama and said simply, "I love Granny."

Mama bent over and kissed Elizabeth's forehead. "I do too," she said fervently. "We all do."

I crawled into bed with my sisters, but I couldn't seem to fall asleep as fast as they did. Even Mama was already drawing the slow and even breaths of sleep as she lay in the big bed with Eva. I kept thinking about that rocking chair rocking all by itself. It had made Mama so happy, and then there was that strange warm feeling that had made me cry, but I'd felt happy, too.

I turned over to get more comfortable, wondering if Papa had made it to Spring City yet. I felt kind of sorry for him. When he got there, all he would see was Granny's body. We were lucky to have been left behind, because we had been able to be in the same room as her spirit.

Eventually I got tired of thinking, and my eyelids got heavy. When they closed, I felt the brush of a gentle hand on my head, the kind of touch that would come from a beloved Granny. I was too tired to open my eyes, but I didn't need to. I wore a contented smile as my mind slipped easily into sleep.

*Adelaide Sahlberg Thompson told this story to her niece, Vida Sorensen, before Adelaide's death in 1981. While living on a flat outside of the town of Ferron, Utah, in 1899, Adelaide's mother Hannah received word that her own mother, Margareta Persson Sandstrom, had died in Spring City. Hannah wanted desperately to go to the funeral, but was disappointed when her husband Edmund firmly told her "no." He immediately left to attend the funeral himself.*

*That evening, after family prayers, Adelaide and her sisters stared in disbelief as the old rocking chair began to rock of its own accord. Her mother explained that their grandmother had chosen to use her favorite old rocker to say goodbye, since they hadn't been able to go to the funeral. Adelaide was soothed and calmed by the experience (Saga of the Sanpitch, Vol. 14, pg. 17).*

# SHADOW OF DEATH

Josine's frantic breathing rasped across my nerve ends, pulling me up rigid on the edge of my chair. Her fingers dug into my hand, signaling that another pain was coming. She pierced my heart with a desperate look just before arching her back and screaming again. Her voice came out raspy and ghost-like from a throat worn down by repeated outcries that brought no relief. She pushed her huge belly up off the bed, garbled cries of anguish coming weakly between quick gasps for air.

"Jo," I said desperately, "I've got to get help."

It didn't seem possible, but my wife's grip on my fingers tightened. She shook her head from side to side and whimpered, letting me know that the pain was finally beginning to let up some. "Don't leave me," she gasped. Her tortured eyes searched my face, begging for reassurance.

I rubbed the back of her hand. "But you've been laboring for so long," I said. "I'm worried."

"Don't leave," she begged again, her eyes clinging to mine.

I pressed the back of her hand up to my lips and kissed it. "I won't go," I assured her. Josine closed her eyes and sank her head back into the pillow. She lay so limp and pale that she could have been dead. I reached out to caress her cheek and felt the ghost of a breath on my hand.

I knew it wouldn't be long before another pain would grip my young wife's body and wrench her up in another spasm of agony. What could I do? I glanced toward the window of our little house and saw the same thing I'd seen the last time I looked. Snow. Cold flakes were falling to the ground as fast as grain pouring from a bucket, so thick you couldn't even see the tree next to our house.

This was all my fault. Since Jo had been a little nervous about expecting our first child, she wanted to look at houses in town when we first moved here a few months ago. I was the one

9

who convinced her that we should build a house on our own homestead. As I painted her a picture with words, I could see in my own mind our strong and vibrant sons running through fields of tall grain, playing hide and seek among the rows of corn. Our rosy-cheeked daughters would help Jo plant flowers and push each other on the swing I'd hang from that straight limb of the box elder tree in our yard. Our children would, by necessity, become one another's best friends. We would be a close, happy family, tied to our land by birth and tradition.

I had been overjoyed when Josine had finally relented. She hadn't even complained that our finished cabin was only one room. She had been content with my promise to add on as the children came along.

Now I could kick myself clear across the farm. Why hadn't I seen that it would be better for Jo to be in a house in town, where we would have neighbors to help her, and a doctor within walking distance? An arrow of guilt shot through me, splintering in pain at the very core of my being. I wished mightily that I could take the hurt from Josine and put it all on myself. I would rather have suffered everything she was feeling than to watch her go through it.

"Dear God, please help us," I whispered as I felt Jo's fingers tighten on my hand once again. Too soon, she was caught up in another battle with her body, her face twisted so that I hardly recognized her. I tried rubbing her arm as she thrashed and screamed, but she slapped at my hand, too caught up in the pain to even speak.

"Josine, what can I do?" I asked hopelessly as she relaxed uneasily back into her pillow, her face wet with tears and sweat.

"Make it stop," she said in a small, scared voice.

Tears welled up in my eyes. "I don't know how," I said, my heart aching for my wife.

"I feel like I'm going to die," she whispered just before she closed her eyes and slumped into an unnatural quiet.

My heart caught. "Josine?" I said. She didn't answer. Even her breathing was silent. A chill warning seized me, kicking my heart into a panic. I checked Jo for breathing, but her belly dwarfed everything else about her. I put my hand up to her face, but I felt no fluttering breath.

"Don't die!" I yelled, standing up and grabbing her shoulders.

Josine slowly opened her eyes, as though it took great effort. Her distant gaze finally found me. "I don't want to," she said, drawing out her words as though she had to think hard to find them in her brain. "I just want...our baby." Her eyes fell closed again. Alarmed, I pulled my wife's hand up and cradled it against my chest, the feel of her warm skin a lifeline in my hands. What could I do? I'd never felt so alone and afraid in my life.

A sudden blast of cold air hit my back. I whirled around to face the opening door. To my amazement, a rotund man of medium height with cheeks buffed red by the cold stepped inside my house, followed by a barrage of snowflakes. He turned and leaned against the door, forcing it closed. As soon as he caught sight of me, he gave me a delighted smile that did nothing to ease the tension in the room. Who did he think he was? What was he doing barging in here?

To my chagrin, he took off his hat and dusted it against his pant leg, sending a shower of snowflakes onto the plank floor. Anger flooded my chest. This was my home and my family, and I would stand between them and this intruder. I took a step toward the stranger. "What are you . . ." I began gruffly. My challenge was cut off by the dreaded pressure of Josine's fingers on my hand. Another pain was swelling up inside her. My nerves stretched taut with worry over Jo and my need to confront the unwelcome stranger.

I couldn't just tear myself from Josine's grasp and abandon her to strain against the force that was wrenching the life out of her. I kept my eyes locked on the stranger as he hurried over to our table and set a black leather bag on top. He glanced over at Jo as he shrugged out of his snow-spattered coat and hung it on the back of a chair. Josine was screaming, writhing in a futile effort to escape the pain that was at the very center of her being. The stranger turned away from us and helped himself to the water in our wash basin. He scrubbed his hands and shook them out in the air as Josine's screams faded to sobs.

"Who are you?" I demanded.

"Doctor Konig," the man declared proudly, seeming delighted to be able to introduce himself at last.

My anger gave way to astonishment, then gratitude. *Thank you*, I breathed to the heavens. My knees buckled in relief and I sagged down into my chair. It had to have been guidance from above that led the doctor to our door in this blizzard.

Without waiting for an invitation, Doctor Konig strode toward the bed. The broad smile he wore filled me with hope. It was not the face of a man who was looking at imminent death.

"What a happy occasion!" the doctor said. His voice had a guttural sound, an accent that gave away his foreign birth. I wasn't one much for languages, but it sounded like it could be German. "It looks like you're soon to have a sweet little baby here." His tone changed from jovial to firm. "Papa," he said, looking at me.

"Me?" I answered, confused.

The doctor raised his eyebrows. "You are the papa, aren't you?"

"Well, yes," I admitted.

"Get some water boiling," he said as he moved the sheet aside from Josine's legs. "Get me some clean cloths. Do you have a little blanket for your baby?"

I jumped up and pulled my hand out of Josine's. Her eyes flew open in a panic, and she reached for me. I bent over her and smoothed her hair. "It's all right, Jo," I said. "A doctor is here."

It took a moment for her to focus on the jovial face of Doctor Konig. "Hello, Mama," he said with a tender smile. "It looks like maybe your little baby is confused about how it's supposed to come into this world."

"What do you mean?" I asked sharply.

Doctor Konig turned mildly surprised eyes toward me. "Your baby is turned the wrong way." The doctor nodded reassurance. "He's a little mixed up, but I can help him."

Then Doctor Konig frowned at me. "Are you a little mixed up too?" I was confused by his reprimand. "Didn't I ask you to boil some water?" he reminded me sternly.

I hurried over to the stove as Josine's voice raised into a weak wail. Another cruel pain had her in its clutches. My heart hurt in sympathy for my wife, yet having Doctor Konig here had blanketed my panic with hope. He would know what to do.

I filled the kettle and pushed it over the fire. As Josine cried out, I spotted some clean cloth and reached out to pick it up. My hands were shaking, and I noticed the distinct prints of Josine's fingers on the back of my hand where she had hung onto me for so long.

My wife's screams subsided again, and I heard Doctor Konig murmuring to her. I hoped that the heavily accented voice was as soothing to Josine as it was to me. I was no longer facing this desperate situation alone. I looked over at Jo, her pale face sunk into the pillow, eyes closed against the thought of the next onslaught of pain, and my heart nearly burst with sorrow and love.

"Come, hold her hands," Doctor Konig commanded me. "I must turn the baby." I hurried over to my wife's side and held firmly to her hands as if it would keep her from slipping away into the next world without me. The doctor did what had to be done. Josine struggled and cried, but I held her. "I love you, Jo. I won't leave you, ever," I murmured close to her ear. "Now you'll be fine. The baby will be fine. Our baby, Josine, our sweet little baby. You're so brave. I love you so much." I kept it up until Doctor Konig called out cheerfully, "Push, Mama, push your little baby out. Papa, go get the water."

I hurried to the kitchen, grabbed the kettle, and started back toward the doctor. He saw me coming and shook his head. "Put it in a basin," he said. I turned around to do his bidding, my face hot with frustration at my inability to be a good midwife.

13

In spite of my inexperienced help, in a blessedly short time Josine gave a last mighty push and Doctor Konig held up a wrinkly red baby for our inspection. "Congratulations, you have a son," he announced. He went about cutting the cord and wiping the new little body clean with warm water. Tears stung my eyes as my baby wailed in hearty protest.

Doctor Konig wrapped the tiny boy snugly in a piece of clean flannel, which quieted his lusty cries. "Here, Papa," he said, setting the little bundle gently into my arms. "I still need to help Mama for a minute. You get acquainted with your son until I am finished."

I stared down into the little face that tried mightily to keep his eyes open, but could only manage little peeks against the brightness of the world from between tiny little eyelids. His mouth twisted up into a toothless grimace, and he let out a soft squall. I bounced him gently up and down, my heart overflowing with love for this new little boy.

It wasn't long before Josine was ready to reach for our son and hold him in a tender embrace, her eyes now brimming with tears of joy instead of pain. I circled my new little family in my arms, marveling at the miracle of this baby boy that Josine and I had made together. I also marveled at Josine's new disposition. Although pale, she was smiling, no longer hovering over the precipice of death.

Quietly the door closed. I spun around and saw that the room was empty. The doctor's bag was gone, too. I jumped up and ran to the door. Flinging it open, I called, "Doctor Konig! Come back!" The snow was thinning enough that I could see between the flakes out to the road, but there was no one there. "At least let us give you something warm to drink!" I called. Silence.

Perplexed and disappointed, I turned back into the house to care for my wife and son. My son. The realization that I had a son warmed me like a fire in my heart.

A week or so later, I saddled up and rode through the deep snowfall, making tracks along the smooth white trail as I headed into town. The first place I stopped was the doctor's office. No one answered my knock, so I stepped into the hotel next door to see if they knew where the doctor was.

After the clerk greeted me with a pleasant, practiced smile, my eyes found a picture of Doctor Konig hanging behind the desk. "Where can I find the doctor?" I asked, pointing to the picture.

The clerk turned his head to look behind him. "Doctor Konig?" he asked.

"Yes."

The clerk lost his smile, and his eyes turned somber. "In the graveyard," he said quietly.

"No," I said, my mouth open, my heart dropping in despair. "He can't be dead."

"I'm afraid he is," the clerk said. "It was tragic. Such a kind man."

"What happened?" I asked, deep sorrow stirring my soul into painful regret at the loss of such a good man. The doctor hadn't even mentioned payment for his services.

The clerk shook his head. "His kindness was his undoing."

"How?" I didn't want to believe him.

"It was during last year's epidemic. Doctor Konig kept traveling from house to house, doing everything he could to relieve the suffering. He refused to stop, even when a blizzard came up. He tried to ride through the storm to the next house, but he got lost and finally died from the cold."

My heart seemed to stop beating. "Last year?"

"Yep," the clerk said, leaning forward on his desk. "The whole town was at the funeral. A lot of tears were cried that day, I can tell you.

"It's not possible," I whispered.

The clerk shrugged and stood up straight. He jerked a thumb over his shoulder. "You can go see for yourself. His headstone's in the graveyard, dates carved in it and everything."

The clerk put both palms down on his desk. "We've got a new doc now. He's an all right man for medicine, I suppose, but he doesn't have the same heart that Doctor Konig had."

I nodded mutely. I didn't know what else to say. I turned and wandered back out into the world that was buried under a blanket of snow.

*J. N. Simpson's pioneer mother told this story as one that truly happened. A young couple struggling with the birth of their first baby in a snowstorm on an isolated farm were surprised when a doctor showed up and helped them safely deliver the baby. The next time the husband went into town, he tried to find the doctor to thank him, but was told that the doctor had died a year earlier and was buried in the cemetery. J. N. Simpson wrote the story down in 1976 for the Saga of the Sanpitch, Vol. 8 pg.46.*

# THE FOLLOWER

We bumped our loaded wagon over the rise that gave way to a sloping road, leading down through the valley and into Spring City. From this distance I could see that the leaves on the trees lining the streets of town were still a defiant green, yet I knew it wouldn't be long before the red and orange of the frost-nipped canyon trees would spread downward, overtaking the city and tugging the cold nights and winter snows along behind them.

I pushed my foot down hard on the brake when the wagon picked up speed on the hill. My brother Henry grabbed the edge of the seat. "Easy!" he said.

"Do you want to drive?" I asked him gruffly.

"Just don't run over the horses," he retorted.

"That's what the brake's for," I shot back. I kept my eyes on the team. The horses high stepped in order to keep ahead of the bulky wagon. I stood on the brake and gritted my teeth, leaving the reins slack so the horses could maneuver the heavy load of firewood as best they could until the wagon leveled out on the flat stretch before town. I eased up on the brake and the horses fell back to a walk. I sank back down on the seat.

Henry snorted and relaxed his grip. He leaned back, his arms folded contemptuously over his chest. Not wanting to invite more criticism from my eighteen-year-old brother, I tried to pretend he wasn't there. I leaned forward with my elbows on my knees, studiously ignoring Henry, as aloof and in control as befitted my status of being two years older than him. The reins were loose in my hands, and the warmth from the sun soaked into my back.

I didn't bother trying to start a conversation. It might be enough to spark Henry into a stupid debate over some trivial thing.

I let my mind wander back to the cold bite in the air this morning when Henry had gone with me for a load of firewood.

I'd had to keep wiping at my nose as we'd ridden the empty, rattling wagon up into the frosty canyon. We'd soon warmed ourselves up by felling dead trees.

It was eerie how on the afternoon of the same day, the sun was beating down warm and bright, almost like this was a whole different day. Some things grew hard to believe if you thought about them long enough.

From the corner of my eye, I saw Henry turn toward me. I braced for another complaint, or at best, an earful of constructive criticism. "What the . . ." Henry muttered in a fearful whisper. I turned to stare at him, confused as much by his words as the odd tone of his voice. Henry's face was frozen in a mask of utter disbelief, his eyes wide with dread, staring at something behind me. An icy apprehension washed down my spine.

I turned to look. A horse was approaching us, a dark creature with a broad and well-muscled chest. The rider astride the horse was dressed in an old brown coat and dark trousers, his feet stuck into stirrups and his hands holding the reins. Everything about him looked very ordinary except for one thing—he had no head.

My eyes strained against their sockets, and a cold sweat broke out on my brow. It was impossible. No one without a head could ride a horse. My heart was seized in a painful grip of horror. I tried to call out to my brother, but my throat closed up tight, barely able to draw breath.

The rider moved relentlessly toward us. The easy gait of his mount would surely overtake our heavy wagon. The thought of having him ride up beside me set my heart pounding wildly in an effort to escape. My mouth went dry. When I tried to swallow, I nearly choked. I blinked hard, desperately hoping that what I was seeing was some kind of terrible trick, but blinking did not make the headless rider disappear. He stayed right on course, slowly gaining on us.

"What is that?" Henry's voice, tight with panic, made me jump. Prickles of fright danced along my neck and I threw a terrified glance at my brother.

"I don't know," I answered, my voice sounding strange and distant in my own ears. My frantically pounding heart drowned out all other sounds. "It surely doesn't look natural." When Henry didn't bother to shoot a sarcastic remark at me, I knew he was plenty scared.

As much as it spooked me, I couldn't tear my eyes away from the horrible sight. The dark horse casually angled its way down the slope of the hill, turning the rider sideways. Although I thought I was already as scared as I could possibly be, sick apprehension flooded the pit of my stomach as the rider was sharply outlined in the dying rays of a setting sun. He had absolutely no head anywhere.

Pure panic shot through me. I finally managed to tear my eyes away from the headless thing and I slapped the reins against the backs of the horses. "Giddyup!" I screamed.

Surprised by my wild outcry, the horses jockeyed in their traces before they matched their paces and began pulling the wagon at a faster clip. I threw a glance over my shoulder and was horrified to see the headless horseman kick his mount to greater speed.

"Go faster!" Henry squeaked through teeth bared in terror. I again wildly slapped my poor horses with the reins. They threw back their heads before beginning an awkward gallop. My only thought was to put as much distance as I could between me and the hideous thing that was following us.

I threw a glance over my shoulder and saw the headless rider lean forward. My stomach heaved. I whipped my head forward so I wouldn't have to see where his head had been. "Yaw!" I yelled at the horses. "Is it gaining?" I asked as I shot my forearm up to wipe my sweating forehead. I leaned forward in my seat as if that would somehow make the horses go faster.

"I don't know," Henry gasped, leaning forward beside me, his face the color of whitewash and his eyes two sizes bigger than normal.

"Turn around and see!" I shouted.

Henry flung me a scared, desperate look before he checked behind us. "Looks like he's about the same," Henry said, a quaver in his voice. I risked a glance over my shoulder and saw the headless rider matching the rhythm of his mount's strides. Then he lightly slapped the reins against his horse's neck. I whipped forward and hollered, "Giddyup!"

Henry looked back. "I think he's gaining, Frank," he stuttered. He grabbed my arm in a grip that hurt.

"Let go!" I screamed, and slapped at my brother's hand. I flung a look back and saw that the horseman was indeed closer than the last time I'd looked. My heart pounded so hard it felt like it would burst from my chest. I slapped the reins again, so scared I could barely see.

The sound of heavy breathing sent a shock up my spine. I didn't want to look, but I had to. I jerked my head around and saw the rider nearly caught up to the wagon bed. His horse captured me with his cold eyes, so dark and bottomless that I felt like I was falling.

Henry grabbed a handful of my shirt. "Stay with me!" he screamed as he jerked me back upright. A shiver of dread shook me from head to foot as I realized that I'd nearly tumbled off the seat and onto the road. I wiped the sweat out of my eyes before I stared at the horses laboring mightily to pull the loaded wagon. For the first time since I'd begun this desperate flight from a headless man, I began worrying about the horses. How long could they keep up this insane pace? They had to be slowed before they dropped dead of exhaustion, because then where would we be?

I shot a trembling look over my shoulder. The headless rider trailed a few yards behind the wagon. I turned forward and forced myself to ease back on the reins, my shoulders hunched with dread at the thought of giving the thing behind me a chance to catch up.

"What are you doing?" Henry screamed. He leaned over and jerked at the reins.

"The horses can't keep up this pace," I said, hanging onto the leather strips with all my might, refusing to let my brother pull them away.

"Horses?" Henry hollered. "What about us? Go faster!"

Even though my throat was clogged with fear, I glanced behind me again. The headless rider turned his mount off the road, his shoulders hitching unevenly to match the horse's gait. They moved together at an easy walk toward the town dump. "It's leaving," I said, relief seeping through my tight muscles, loosening their death grip on my bones. My teeth were chattering. I clamped them shut, but tremors still rattled me in spasms.

Henry looked behind us with wide eyes. "What's it doing?" he asked.

I shrugged and shivered. "I don't know, but it's not after us." I pulled back slow and steady on the reins, letting the gasping horses drop back to a walk. I stared over my shoulder as the rider on the dark horse ambled his way into the draw that held the growing pile of refuse from our little town. He rode behind a skimpy clump of brush. I should have been able to see the horse and rider through the spidery branches, but even as I watched, all movement ceased. Although I kept my eyes on the shrubbery for a long time, nothing came out the other side.

"What was that thing?" Henry hollered as he seized my shoulder.

"I don't know!" I said, my heart attempting to resume its normal pace. I shrugged out from under his hand.

Henry sat staring with unseeing eyes at the road as it led us inevitably into town. He glanced back one more time at the empty landscape behind us before he leaned in toward me. "Maybe that's the same thing," he said in a voice that still trembled.

"The same thing as what?" I asked, not sure I wanted to know.

"You know, the thing that caused the old Ephraim Cemetery to be where it is," he whispered ominously. The skin on his face was sickly white.

Shade thrown across the road from trees that lined the street blocked the sun and chilled the air, raising goosebumps along the flesh of my arms. "How could that thing put a cemetery anywhere?" I scoffed, hoping that the false bravado in my voice would chase the shivers out of my bones.

"You haven't heard?" Henry asked, his eyes wide with fear and knowing. "You remember when old Ed McKnight's dad was killed by Indians?"

"I wasn't there at the time," I replied sarcastically, wishing he'd talk about something else.

"Well, yeah, of course not, you weren't even born fifty years ago, but Ed tells me that the two men who found his dad's body were coming back from a run for firewood up in the canyon." Henry glanced back at the fully loaded wagon behind us. "They were shocked to find a dead man along the trail, but they did the decent thing and loaded his body on the wagon. They were about a mile north of town when the wagon broke down, right next to a clump of trees. The men climbed down to fix it. They worked so long that it was full dark by the time they heard the noise."

Henry stopped talking and stared at me as intently as a vulture watching a creature die. Perched on the edge of my seat, it felt as though my nervous system was trying to crawl out of my skin. "What noise?" I asked.

"The sound of hooves," Henry answered slowly. "Horse's hooves moving around in the dark." Henry's voice lowered to a whisper. "They were sure it was the Indians, come back to add two more scalps to their lodge." Henry paused again.

"Well, was it?" I demanded.

"What?"

"Indians! Was it Indians?"

Henry put a cold hand on my arm. "It was too dark to see. By the time the hoof beats faded away, the two men were scared nearly out of their wits. They were decent enough to dig a shallow grave right on the spot, then they laid Ed's dad in it. They claim to have said a prayer over him, but I think they were praying for their own safety as they covered him up. They unhitched the team, swung up onto the horses, and high-tailed it for the fort as fast as they could move in the dark." Henry's fingers gripped me tighter. "But do you know what, Frank?"

"What?" I snapped, wishing he would just tell me the whole story all at once.

"Indians don't travel at night, on account of they're scared of evil spirits."

"Yeah, so?"

"So it couldn't have been Indians they heard riding in the night." Henry threw his thumb over his shoulder, jabbing in the direction we'd just come from. "But it could have been him."

Henry's words sunk into me like ice water from a mountain stream. As I turned in by our house, the cold settled in enough to make me shiver as the sun hid itself behind the mountains. As soon as we unhitched the horses and put them in the barn, I headed past the wagon. Grabbing an armload of dried branches that we'd stuffed in around the logs, I went in to the house and knelt in front of the fireplace. I laid a fire directly over the ashes from the morning. Blowing on the coals, I soon had a blaze going and sat myself plumb in front of it, trying to soak up heat that couldn't reach far enough to thaw the cold in my bones.

*Joseph Franklin Hansen told his grandchildren that on more than one occasion, a headless horseman followed him and his brother down from the canyon east of Spring City when they went to cut wood in the early part of the 20th Century. Although the story was met with skepticism by grandson Quay Hansen, who says it sounds like an old wives' tale, he also admits that his grandfather never told the story with less than a totally serious demeanor, and never confessed that the tale was any kind of fabrication.*

*There is a legend that the first grave in the Ephraim Pioneer Cemetery was dug by a couple of men transporting a body.*

*They were spooked by unexplained noises. Afraid of an Indian attack, they performed a hasty burial before hurrying to the safety of the fort in town. When more bodies were added beside the lonely grave, the old Ephraim Cemetery was established.*

# TWO TICKETS, PLEASE

Someone cleared his throat loudly, and I turned to see who it was. Framed in the train station window was the scowling face of Jorgen Nielsen.

"Why, Brother Nielsen," I said kindly. A man who had just lost his wife deserved some sympathy. "I'm so sorry about Anne Marie."

Jorgen cast his eyes down for a moment and nodded his thanks. Then he spoke without looking up. "I want two tickets to Fountain Green," he mumbled.

"What?" I asked.

Jorgen lifted his head and stared defiantly into my eyes. "Two tickets," he said, "to Fountain Green."

I leaned my elbows on the little window ledge at the ticket window. "Why do you want them?" I asked. "With your wife's funeral in just three days, why would you be leaving? And two tickets? Who are you taking to Fountain Green?"

Jorgen's jaw shot forward. "That is none of your business."

Undisturbed by his outburst, I held my ground and studied his face. Although it didn't happen often, sometimes the grief from losing a wife would throw a man into an unbalanced state of mind.

Jorgen stared back at me for a long moment, his chest heaving as he challenged my gaze. Finally he spoke. "Well?"

"Well?" I answered him.

Jorgen thumped one fist on the counter. "It is my business," he insisted. "Maybe I'll tell you later, maybe I won't. Just make out the tickets!"

I figured that any more questioning on my part would only make matters worse. Besides, as station master, I would be here when the train left, and I would see what was what. I pulled out the necessary forms and filled them out, then took Jorgen's money. I slid the tickets into his waiting hand. He snatched them up and whirled around, nearly bumping into the couple standing behind him in line. They stepped back, their faces startled. "What are you staring at?" he grumped at them. He stomped off through the crowd, earning curious glances from those waiting to board. There were lots of people either waiting to greet someone, or those who simply liked the hustle of a station when a train was due.

I would never have described Jorgen Nielsen as a jovial man, but it was plain to see that his personality had not improved any from the passing of his wife. As I got the tickets for the bewildered couple who had nearly been run over by Jorgen, I wondered how he would get along without his wife. I recalled that the only negative thing I'd ever heard Jorgen say about his Anne Marie was that she would get riled if the chickens or hogs wandered up onto the porch. Otherwise, on the few occasions I heard him speak of her, it was only for good things. He'd say he liked her cooking, or he'd boast that she would get up first on a cold morning and build the fire. Then she would lay his pants out on a chair in front of the flames to warm them before he even crawled out from under the covers.

I was checking the list of tickets I'd sold when I heard the train whistle off in the distance. The people on the platform turned their heads almost as one toward the south. That was when I noticed Otto G. Olsen's hearse pull up to the station, his matched white horses tossing their heads. The train whistle sounded its mournful warning again, and the black plumes on the horse's bridles twitched into a macabre dance.

No one had told me that any caskets were being shipped in today. I felt a bit put out. I prided myself on the ability to keep my finger on the pulse of the community. I was a trusted source of information for those who had questions about comings and goings, events, the weather, and human nature. I didn't like not knowing. Knowing things was part of my job.

The train chugged into the station with a squeal of brakes and the huge pistons on the wheels turning in ever slowing circles. I stepped outside my office. The only reason I could think of for Otto to bring his hearse was to carry some dearly departed to the cemetery for burial. I was mighty curious to see who it was.

When Otto opened the back doors of his hearse wagon, I saw with great consternation that there was a casket inside. I actually couldn't remember a time when anyone who'd died in town had been sent away to be buried anywhere else. The last death I knew of was Anne Marie. My worst suspicions were confirmed when I caught sight of a scowling Jorgen Nielsen standing beside the baggage car.

Otto called to some of the men who were standing and watching the proceedings. "We need some help to lift this casket," he said as he circled his hand toward himself in a rolling motion, inviting approach. "Come, come, grab that corner there, it shouldn't take more than four of you. Anne Marie's not heavy. The good woman had just enough lap for snuggling a child. We need to show some respect and help her along her way." Otto glanced over at Jorgen and added, "Wherever that may be."

I figured I knew where Jorgen was taking her, but if he hadn't told anyone, it wasn't my place to do so yet. Several men had responded to Otto's plea for help and were now sliding the wooden coffin into the train's baggage car. Jorgen stood and watched—his hat in his hands, his jaw clenched. As soon as the casket was settled and the men moved away, Jorgen climbed up into the car and sat on the floor beside the earthly remains of his wife. The door was pushed shut, and the conductor called, "All aboard!"

After a few moments, the train slowly pulled away from the station, picking up speed as it chugged along the track. As soon as the noise had quieted enough that we could hear one another speak, Otto said, "By jingo, why should Brother Jorgen want to take Anne Marie for a ride in the baggage car?"

"And where is he taking her?" asked Jens Sondrup.

"To Fountain Green," I answered. "I sold him the tickets myself."

"Why would they go there?" Otto asked, his shoulders hunched and his hands spread out as though the answer to his question might fall into them from the sky. "People who leave for the city come home to Ephraim for their final resting place, but I don't ever remember anyone going out of town to be buried."

A silence fell over the platform at his words. Was it possible that Jorgen had taken Anne Marie to be buried in a different town? Why?

"He bought two plots in our new graveyard," Otto announced.

After a shocked silence, Jens asked, "Then why? Is he planning to re-marry?"

"But Anne Marie is his first wife," someone else said. "He should be buried beside her. It's only proper."

"If he's not burying her in this cemetery, why buy two plots here?" someone else asked. "That's not very frugal of him." Several of the men shook their heads in disapproval.

The speculation was ended by False Bottom Larsen. "I'll go ask Karen Skrook. Jorgen's own sister ought to know what's going on." He turned on his heel and trotted away. If there was one person that hated not knowing more than I did, it was False Bottom.

Feeling certain of his success in learning the truth, I went back inside the train depot. Knowing False Bottom's fondness for passing a story, I would find out soon enough why Jorgen was taking Anne Marie to Fountain Green.

How was I to know that Karen knew nothing more than the rest of us, except that Anne Marie had grown up in Fountain Green? Jorgen had not revealed his plans to her. Yet it seemed fairly clear that Jorgen intended to lay Anne Marie to rest in the little town she'd grown up in. Why else would he spend perfectly good money for train tickets?

Yet False Bottom made another startling discovery. Jorgen had arranged use of the local meetinghouse for a funeral, even to assigning prayers and talks, and then there were those two cemetery plots he'd bought. Something was going on, but none of us could figure out what.

Two days later, Jorgen returned on the train. Otto again rolled his hearse up to the baggage car. When it opened, Anne Marie's casket was pulled out by some mighty curious volunteers who cast several glances at the steely-faced Jorgen as they loaded the casket back into the hearse.

When people began gathering for the funeral, it was soon apparent that the chapel wouldn't be big enough to hold them all. The bishop suggested moving the funeral into the larger Tabernacle, which was soon filled to capacity with curious townsfolk dressed in their somber best. It was the best attended funeral I'd ever been to.

Once all the nice things were said and Anne Marie was prayed over, we followed the hearse to the cemetery and watched as she was laid to rest in one of the two plots Jorgen had bought.

Having proven that he was no traitor after all, Jorgen received numerous handshakes and heartfelt claps on the back. Several of us followed him home, where the ladies of the Relief Society had filled the table and sideboards with pans and bowls of chicken fricassee, mashed potatoes, sweet soup, dumpling soup, and sweet rolls. There weren't enough places for all of us to sit, but we didn't mind crowding ourselves around the walls, leaning against the wallpaper as we ate our fill and darted glances at Jorgen.

It didn't surprise me that even when people finished eating, they didn't leave. They stood around in groups, whispering among themselves and shooting looks at Jorgen, who sat brooding in his big armchair among pillows sewn by Anne Marie herself. He was studiously avoiding eye contact with anyone. I knew what people were waiting for, and at last I spoke what was on everyone's mind.

"Brother Nielsen," I said solemnly. "At the train station, you said sometime you would tell me why you bought those two tickets and took Anne Marie to Fountain Green." I purposely left off the "maybe," and hoped Jorgen would forget it, too. "Will you tell us now?"

Jorgen glared at the floor, his hands clasped in his lap and his thumbs working themselves around and around each other until I worried that he might wear his skin off. He might ignore my question, but I decided that until those thumbs quit turning, I would wait him out. No one else spoke, not even a whisper. The air of expectation was as thick as the curiosity. All eyes were securely fastened on the widower sitting hunched in his chair.

It was a long few minutes later that Jorgen's thumbs stopped and he bent his elbows to grip the chair arms. His jaw thrust forward and he swept the crowded room with hostile eyes.

"I was not going to say anything about our trip," he blurted out, "but I know you will all pester me and pester me like horse-flies at haying time until you find out what you want to know. And what you want to know is none of your business. It is only for my own peace of mind that I will tell you, but I will only say it once."

Jorgen let go of the chair arms and relaxed back against the upholstery with an air of resignation. "Not many of you know that Anne Marie grew up in Fountain Green. She still has friends and family there, so I thought it would be nice if I took her to them so they would not have to make the trip to Ephraim." Jorgen raised his eyes and looked at the undertaker. "They all said how nice Otto made Anne Marie look," he said. "All day long people came to the house where Anne Marie used to live. Her mother and father were happy to have her there. We had a little meeting, almost like a funeral, before I brought her back here to Ephraim."

Jorgen sat silent for another minute, but sensing that the story wasn't complete, we all held our places. Jorgen looked sideways up at us, then sighed. "The best thing about that train trip to Fountain Green was that I didn't have to have her family come stay here with me. Besides her father and mother there are four brothers, so wide they could be mistaken for oxen on a dark road in the night. And Anne Marie has two sisters who are so big they'd render out two crocks of lard each. All of them eat like Ras Knap's big Percheron horses in plowing time. Besides those there are also twenty or thirty of the small ones. If I had to feed all those in that family, it would have been like when the grasshoppers swarmed over the fields last summer. There wouldn't likely have been one scrap of food left in the whole town, and maybe not in Manti, either."

I hid a smile behind my hand and noticed other men nodding their approval at Jorgen's explanation. Those closest to the door stepped through to the outside, and were followed by a steady stream of townspeople, their curiosity satisfied and their tongues wagging. Jorgen was finally left in peace.

*In the 1989 edition of* Saga of the Sanpitch *on page 100, Woodruff C. Thomson of Provo, Utah, gives thanks and apologies to Chris Jensen, "Sheepherder Sam," for his story "Take Her Home to Her Family; Don't Bring Them to Her,"* The Salt Lake Tribune, *July, 1975, page A-3.*

*According to the* Saga *account, Jorgen Nielson bought two tickets to Fountain Green from Ephraim, Utah for himself and the body of his newly deceased wife. He refused to tell anyone why he was taking his wife's body for a ride. He returned two days later with the casket. Partly out of curiosity, there followed one of the best-attended funerals the valley had ever seen. When it was over, Jorgen admitted that he had taken her to Fountain Green so that her numerous family members could pay their respects. With brothers as big as oxen and sisters that would "render two crocks of lard each," he had avoided having to play host. Since the account mentions that Anne Marie was laid to rest in the new Park Cemetery, this incident must have taken place around 1901.*

# HORSE ON A HILL

I wished that Mama hadn't made me come with her. She didn't even ask if I wanted to come. I didn't. I wanted to help Papa build our new cabin. Now he had to build it all by himself because Mama was listening to some men who were standing around talking and talking and talking. I could have helped Papa. After all, I was almost four years old. But Mama said, "No, Hyrum, you're coming with me."

One of the men pointed toward the mountains again. There was a lot of pointing going on this morning. Some pointed at the mountains and some pointed at the sagebrush covered valley or the foothills, but no one was doing anything. It was terribly boring.

When I tugged impatiently on Mama's hand, she bent and lifted me up. I didn't want to be held, I wanted to play, so I wiggled to get down. She held me tighter. "Hold still," she whispered.

"Mama, can't we go now?" I asked.

"Not yet," she answered, before putting her finger to her lips. She listened to more talk about temples and Brother Brigham. I sighed and laid my head on her shoulder, trying to get comfortable. There were a few other ladies standing and listening, but mostly there were men.

I wished that all the talking people would just say, "Amen." That word means you can leave the meeting.

I stared longingly toward our dugout. It was on the sunny side of the tall hill that pushed out from the side of the east mountain range into the Sanpitch valley. Even if Mama hadn't wanted me to help Papa this morning, she could have let me stay in the dugout. I could have rolled my ball across the dirt floor. If I rolled it hard enough, it would bounce off the willow branches that Mama had woven together and pushed up against the walls to try to cover the dirt. If I hit the branches just right, my ball would bounce off and roll back to me so that I didn't even have to go chasing it.

The thought of playing with my ball made me all wiggly and impatient, so Mama set me down on the ground. "Shush, Hyrum," she said as she took a firm hold of my hand. I didn't think it was fair of her to shush me when I hadn't even said anything.

My legs were itching to run and play, but I knew it wouldn't work to try to pull on Mama's hand. She was scared that either a rattlesnake might bite me or that I would wander off and the Indians might take me. I used to be scared of things like that, too, but right now I felt like I'd rather be carried off and taken anywhere but here. I didn't see how I could possibly hold still for one more minute.

I leaned against Mama's skirt and looked around to see if I could spot Papa. I couldn't see him anywhere over by the cabins that were rising from the valley floor, so I let my restless eyes wander back to the hill.

When I was a grown up, I would never make my kids wait for me while I talked and talked and talked. No, sir. I wouldn't be a long talker, either. I'd say very little, but I'd do a lot of fun things. Other people could do the talking. When I had little boys, I'd take them with me to build cabins, and never make them listen to boring speakers.

A movement on top of the hill caught my eyes. I looked up and saw a man on a horse as white as old Brother Graham's beard. No, it was whiter than that. It was as white as shining clean and crystally snow without any foot marks in it.

The gleaming horse walked easily along the edge of the hill, carrying a man on its back. At first I wondered if a curious Indian had ridden up there to look down on our meeting. I tipped my hat up so I could see better. That was no Indian up there. The man on the horse was cleaner than anyone I had ever seen in my life. He was dressed all in perfectly white clothes that glowed softly, like moonlight, and fell in cloudy-soft folds around him, rippling lightly as he rode.

He pulled his magnificent horse to a stop. Wondering who he might be, I looked closely at his face. When I found his eyes, my heart gave a mighty jump. He was looking right at me with an expression of such love that I felt wrapped up in warmth more comforting than Mama's big, soft quilt. His smiling eyes were warmer and more welcoming than a woodstove in the kitchen after walking through deep snow for miles and miles.

I couldn't look away from him. I didn't even want to. What I wanted to do was run up the hill and wrap my arms around him. In three steps I was stretched as far as I could be toward him, tugging on Mama's hand that wouldn't let go.

Mama bent down. "Hyrum, hold still," she said.

"Look!" I called, pointing. Mama turned her eyes to see, then slowly straightened, her eyes pinned to the figure on the hill. As we watched, the smiling man and his pure white horse became pale and ghosty looking, like they were being swallowed in a fog. Then they just faded away. Gone.

*No!* my spirit cried in silent anguish. An empty hollowness overtook my heart. I didn't want him to go. I tried to call, "Come back!" but no sound came out of my mouth. Even though I was a big boy, I couldn't stop the hot, disappointed tears. I wanted to go with the man even more than I wanted to be with Papa. It was so strange, the mixed feelings inside, lonely and homesick, while at the same time still glowing warm from the man's smile.

"Did you see that?" Mama asked, sort of quiet. I couldn't answer. My voice still wouldn't work.

"See what?" One of the other ladies turned toward Mama.

"The man dressed in white, riding his horse up on the hill," Mama said, pointing.

The other woman looked up. "I don't see anyone."

"He was there a second ago," Mama said. "He just disappeared."

The other lady was quiet for a moment as she stared at the empty hilltop. Several of the other women who'd heard Mama turned their faces to look at the empty expanse of hill.

The other lady said thoughtfully, "Betsy, if you truly saw a man in white riding across that hill, it could only have been the angel Moroni, coming to tell us that this is the place to put the temple."

"Angel Moroni?" one of the men asked.

Several voices began talking at once, asking what had happened, telling each other what Mama had said. Finally, one voice called out louder than the rest, "Who else saw it?"

Everyone fell silent. Mama glanced from face to face, then bent and lifted me up. "Hyrum did," she said.

A bearded man lowered his eyebrows and stared closely at me. "Did you see the Angel Moroni riding a horse up on that hill, young man?" he asked.

I stared back into his eyes. "No," I said.

Some people in the crowd gasped, others snickered, and some just smiled smugly. Mama's mouth opened in surprise. Before she could say anything, I finished my answer. "It was the Lord."

*Gerald Henrie, great-grandson of Betsy Bradley, relates this experience from Chapter Five of the book* Descendants of William Henrie *by Manetta Prince Henrie. In the spring of 1850, Isaac Morley and others were discussing places to recommend to President Brigham Young for building a temple. Betsy Bradley and her three-year-old son Hyrum saw a white horse ridden by a personage dressed all in white appear on the hill northeast of the new settlement of Manti, then watched in amazement as horse and rider disappeared.*

*People who heard of their experience speculated that it was the angel Moroni, who is said to have dedicated the hill for the building of a temple while he was on the earth. Young Hyrum discounted this opinion with his own. "It was the Lord," he said firmly.*

# BEST FRIENDS

Six-year-old Marian skipped across the grass toward me, the sun brushing her cheeks with pink and making her deep blue eyes sparkle. When she reached my chair set underneath the cottonwood tree, my only daughter perched her little hands on my knee. "Myrtle asked me to play," she announced breathlessly. "May I, Mama? Oh, please say 'yes!'"

I looked into the eyes of my miracle child. I couldn't keep from reaching out to touch her honey brown hair. Standing where she was, the leaves in the tree above us shifted and dappled Marian's hair with spots of sunlight that made her look like a fragile fawn. Marian was beautiful. A rush of gratitude filled my heart. Marian was not my only child, but she was by far the youngest. My three sons had married and made me a grandmother seven times over. My husband Joseph spoiled this only daughter who had blessed our old age. He fed her peppermints and licorice whips. She loved her Papa and was the first to greet him when he came home.

"May I please, Mama?" Marian asked again, this time clasping her hands hopefully in front of her chest. It was such an endearing gesture, this pleading that looked like prayer, that I couldn't resist her.

"All right," I relented. "But be careful."

The radiant smile my little daughter gave me in thanks was worth more than any treasure on earth. She bounced away from me toward Myrtle, who clapped her hands in glee as Marian approached. They linked arms and moved off across the grass.

I stared after them with an unexpected catch in my heart. Ever since I'd known I was carrying Marian in my womb, I'd had a strange, bittersweet feeling that this precious child wasn't going to be mine for very long. I couldn't talk to Joseph about it, because he became terribly agitated if I ever mentioned the possibility of Marian dying before we did.

36

Of course I didn't want anything to take our little daughter from us, but as the years went by, I could never completely shake the feeling that Marian was here on borrowed time. I held each day precious, never sure if it would be Marian's last. Yet she positively radiated life and good health. How could anything happen to her?

With her own brothers so much older, I was glad that Marian had found a friend in little Myrtle Larsen. Myrtle was just turning seven, and the two girls were nearly inseparable. If my daughter wasn't at my house, I could be sure to find her at Myrtle's. Myrtle was a brown haired girl, thin and lively, with an adventurous spirit that sometimes worried me. Yet Myrtle loved to laugh and have fun, her good humor was contagious, and I liked to see Marian giggling with her friend. They were learning their letters, and were ecstatic that both of their names began with "M." They'd recently discovered that they each had six letters in their names. "That makes us twins!" they had exclaimed to me one day, their faces beaming with nearly identical smiles.

From far away, I could hear Myrtle's voice call, "Marian!" searching for my daughter. A sense of unease coursed through me. I sat up and looked in the direction the girls had gone. Was something wrong? Or were they simply playing hide and seek? I tried to stand so I could check on my daughter, but I couldn't get out of my chair. I struggled against whatever unseen force was holding me down as the call came again. "Marian!" Dread rose in my heart, and I struggled all the more, an animal sound of frustration mingled with fear escaping my throat.

"Carrie!" my friend Christiana soothed me.

"Help me!" I begged. I felt a hand on my shoulder and looked up to see Christiana's face. I blinked in confusion at the darkness behind her, and then looked around to see that I was sitting in a rocking chair in my own bedroom. In spite of the single lit lamp, it was alarmingly dark after the sunshine of my dream.

"What time is it?" I asked, panic rising in my chest. I turned and looked toward my bed. My heart sank to see the small figure of Marian, her eyes closed underneath bangs mixed with sweat and stuck to her pale little brow. Her mouth was open and she breathed shallowly. Marian was gripped in the clutches of the dreaded fever. I wished I could go back to my dream, back to the meadow where Marian and Myrtle played together, healthy and laughing.

My heart stopped pounding and slowed to sorrowful rhythm. My premonition that Marian wasn't long for this world loomed large and unwelcome in my breast.

"It's four o'clock in the morning," Christiana told me.

The paralysis from my dream faded away, letting me rise from my chair. I walked over to my daughter's side and touched her hot forehead with my hand. "Did she call out?" I asked.

"No. She's been resting peacefully," Christiana said. She cocked her head to one side. "You cried out in your sleep. Are you all right?"

I nodded wearily. "I had a bad dream," I admitted.

Christiana looked out the screen door into the dark of the summer night. "It's no wonder," she said. Her voice was heavy with the collective sorrow that ran through our town. "This fever is taking so many lives." Christiana glanced back at me, then flicked her eyes to Marian. "It seems especially hungry for little children."

I gripped my daughter's hand, warding off Christiana's words, a tenuous hope threading through my heart that maybe by keeping hold of Marian, she couldn't be taken from me.

Christiana moved toward me and touched my shoulder. "I'm sorry. I shouldn't have said that," she apologized. "Marian's going to be just fine."

I shook my head, but couldn't speak. Christiana's words of reassurance refused to plant themselves in my heart. Instead, they sent needles of pain into my soul that came out as tears. "I don't want her to go," I whispered miserably.

Christiana sat on the bed and put her arms around me. Her touch infused me with the comfort that at least I wasn't alone. I dared to let myself hope that Marian might make it through this bout of fever. After all, other children had recovered. Joseph was out even now, ministering to those in town who were sick and suffering. I hoped he would come home soon, but as soon as the thought entered my mind, I wished him to stay away. I didn't know how strong he would be if this was Marian's last night on earth. With aching heart, I leaned forward and gathered my daughter in my arms, not lifting her off the bed, but holding her gently where she lay.

A whispered name seized my ears. "Marian!"

I released my hold on my daughter and whirled around to face the door. "Did you hear that?"

Christiana's face creased in perplexity. "Hear what?" she asked.

"Someone called Marian," I said.

"Now, Carrie," Christiana reassured me, "only you and I are here. Maybe you'd better try to get more sleep. I'll sit up."

"No," I said, my muscles tight with expectancy. "Listen." We sat in silence for a long moment. I was beginning to doubt my own sanity when the child's voice came again.

"Marian!" The voice was still soft, but now sounded closer and more insistent. Prickles ran up my arms and darted into my heart.

"You must have heard that!" I said. I looked pleadingly into Christiana's face.

Eyes puzzled, Christiana turned toward the doorway. Slowly she made her way out of the bedroom and to the front window. I could see her through the open bedroom door as she stood for a moment, her eyes searching the darkness outside. Suddenly her hand flew to cover her heart. "Oh," was all she said, a small ghost of a whisper.

"What is it?" I asked, my heart catching. Christiana didn't answer. She stared out into the night as though she had been turned to stone. I left my daughter's side and hurried out of the room to join Christiana. I glanced back once to reassure myself that I could still see my daughter before I looked out the window.

Out in the dark night was a sight that made my knees crumple. I grabbed onto the window frame to keep myself upright. Moving solemnly along my front walk was a procession of children. They glided silently toward my front door, looking neither left or right, but fixing their shadowed eyes on my house with an unchildlike intensity of purpose. Each of them carried a lighted candle clutched in their pale fingers.

My first thought was that these children should not be out wandering the roads in the dark hours of early morning. I would never allow Marian to go out this time of night. When I focused my frightened gaze on the child who was leading the procession, my heart lurched in disbelief. The flickering candle flame lit up the unmistakable features of Myrtle Larsen.

No. It was out of the question. Myrtle was in bed with the fever, just like Marian. She couldn't possibly have recovered by now. Yet the child looked so much like her. A chill of fear crawled slowly across the back of my neck.

The light from Myrtle's candle showed a new candle, clutched in her other hand, pale white against her rumpled nightgown. A sudden yet implausible explanation burst into my mind. Perhaps Myrtle had been seized with delirium and gotten out of bed to wander outside without her mother knowing. But what about all the other children? Surely they couldn't all escape their homes and the watchful eyes of their parents. And since when did children voluntarily walk in an orderly row without talking and jostling each other?

Myrtle reached our screen door. I expected to see it open to allow Myrtle to step inside. The door didn't move, but Myrtle walked in anyway. "Marian," she called. With a start, I recognized her voice as the one from my dream. My hair stood on end.

"Myrtle?" I said.

Myrtle didn't look at me, but walked straight toward the bedroom where Marian lay. "I have a candle," Myrtle said hollowly. "I need a light for Marian."

I couldn't force my feet to move as Myrtle leaned over my little daughter, so still and helpless. Myrtle touched the flame of the lighted candle to the wick of the other. The flickering light danced around her strangely gleeful face. She looked as though I'd just told her that Marian could come out and play.

In spite of my spirit whispering to me that what I was seeing wasn't of this earth, I didn't like Myrtle leaning over the bed with the lighted candle. She wasn't old enough to understand the danger. The bedspread might catch fire.

The wick of the new candle suddenly burst into flame. Marian jerked up in bed, abruptly wakened. I put my hand out toward her, wanting to reassure her that Mama was near so she wouldn't be afraid. Before I could even call her name, she collapsed back against the pillows.

I shot a horrified look at Christiana. She was staring through the bedroom door, her eyes riveted on the scene I had just witnessed. I turned and ran for the bedroom, my feet finally obeying as I headed for my daughter's bedside.

Myrtle had vanished. There were no silent children waiting outside. Marian lay still, not the slightest sound coming from her small body. I knew before I even got to her side that she was gone, yet she was warm in my arms when I gathered her to my breast, her head hanging back limply until I pulled it up and tucked it into my shoulder. Silent tears wrung from my heart and rolled down my cheeks. I held my daughter's empty body and shook with grief.

Heavy footsteps sounded on the porch. The screen door flew open and Joseph called out, "Carrie!" but I couldn't answer him. He paused a moment before I heard him say, "Oh, Christiana. I just came from the Larsen's. Little Myrtle died at four o'clock this morning. Marian will be heartbroken."

*Arlea Howell told this story from an experience related by her grandmother as one that happened to Arlea's great grandmother, Christiana Larsen, who was a handcart pioneer. As Christiana sat one night with a neighbor's sick daughter, who was the only girl and the last born by several years, a procession of candle-bearing children came silently to the front door* *in the dark and early hours of morning. The girl's best friend walked through the closed door, leaving the other children outside, and lit a candle over the sick bed. The sick girl abruptly sat up, then fell back on the pillows. The ghost children vanished, and the mother found that her daughter's spirit had indeed left this world. Christiana later found out that the girl's friend had died at the same hour the ghostly children had appeared (*Saga of the Sanpitch, *Vol. 1, pg. 12).*

# HORSE TRADERS

Skittering footsteps sounded behind me in the darkness. I twirled in alarm, my skirt wrapping itself around my ankles at the suddenness of my movement. It straightened itself out before catching a slight breeze. "What was that?" I asked, straining my eyes against a darkness relieved only by a half-moon.

"It was just the wind blowing some old leaves around," John said.

Loyal grabbed my arm, and I about jumped out of my skin. "I see something!" he hissed into my ear. His exclamation shoved my heart up against my ribs like a prisoner straining against iron jail bars.

"You do not!" I whispered back, my eyes searching the darkness that pinned us to the trail.

"It's something black," he said, his voice low with fear. "Up in the tree."

I gave a quick look upward. The moon sent silver-gray beams of light sifting through the tree branches overhead, creating pockets of blackness in every fork and cluster of dead leaves. "It's all black, you ninny," I retorted, my voice shaking.

"It's gonna get you!" Loyal said, digging his fingers into my sides. I screamed before I clamped a hand over my mouth and slapped his hands away. I moved closer to John. He turned and shushed me.

"It was Loyal," I said darkly.

John scowled at me. "Loyal didn't scream, Miranda, that was you," he said. "If you can't be quiet, just go home."

"I can be quiet. It's Loyal that needs to be quiet," I grumped.

John leaned over and put a hand behind his ear. With exaggerated patience he whispered, "I didn't hear anything but you."

I folded my arms against my chest, more from indignation than because I was cold, although the autumn air bit at my ears.

43

At first I'd been excited to be included by my friends in this prank on John's father, who believed wholeheartedly in bad spirits roaming around on this night of All Hallow's Eve. It was easy to laugh at Brother Pettingill's fears in the broad light of day. Now that the dark had chased away the sun and its warmth, I was more willing to admit that there could be some truth in his belief that there were spirits roaming about. There was something in this dark night that twisted things around to unnatural proportions.

I wondered why the boys had really invited me to come. They could have done this by themselves. I thought they'd asked me because we were friends. Now I wasn't sure.

My head snapped up in alarm as a sudden thought struck me. They could be planning to play a prank on me. Perhaps all this business about a joke on John's father wasn't real. Maybe they were taking me to some wild and forsaken place only to abandon me, leaving me to find my own way home. I frowned into the darkness. They wouldn't really do that. They couldn't. They were my friends.

I narrowed my eyes at John. As far as I could tell, he wasn't looking at me anymore. I turned to see what Loyal was doing. His pasty pale face was pointed at me, and he gave me a big, toothy grin, as fake as Brother Jacobson's peg leg. I smiled back. Well, if they were up to something, I was wise to them.

I kept my guard up all the way to Pettingill's barn. So far, so good. There were no lights showing through the windows of the two-story house. John pulled open one of the big barn doors. I stepped inside ahead of Loyal, the warmth of the barn enveloping me like a pair of welcoming arms. It had the comforting smell of animals and hay. The cows were quiet, but I heard a soft nicker come from the far wall.

"Hey, Tub," John said. From where I stood, I could see John's silhouette in the stall window as he stroked a horse's muzzle. It snuffled into his hand affectionately. Another horse swung its head around and blew into John's hair. "Are you

44

jealous, Tilbet?" John laughed. He turned and said, "Loyal, come here and grab Tub's halter."

Loyal shuffled forward in the darkness. "Okay, I've got it," he said.

After a little more thumping and bumping, John said, "I've got Tilbet. Let's get going."

Without a horse to hold, I walked ahead and held the barn door while the boys made their way through, the horses clopping along obediently behind them. Even if the boys decided to jump on the animals now and ditch me, I could find my way home. I would be disappointed, but not scared.

The horses moved out through the barn doors, their smooth gray coats reflecting the ghostly silver light. The subtle moon-glow highlighted the muscles on the horse's sleek flanks. Moving into the dark shade of the willow planted beside the corral gate, the horses slid into a realm of shape-shifting dimness. Only their soft and steady hoofbeats kept me from believing they had really and truly become ghost horses right before my eyes. I couldn't help but wonder if this Halloween night really did have a myste-rious power that didn't touch any other day of the year. Tub and Tilbet came out the other side of the moonshade, their silvery tails swishing full and luxuriant, willingly following John and Loyal down the road.

Out of sight of the farmyard, John relieved my worries of being left behind when he helped me up onto Tilbet's broad, gray back. My seat on the big animal's back infused my legs with welcome warmth. John folded his hands into a step for Loyal to put his foot in. After Loyal was boosted up onto Tub, John stood on a rock and swung himself onto the horse behind me.

The three of us rode toward the Bronson's. The family was new, having taken over the old Christiansen farm around harvest time. Loyal had gone with his father one day to meet the newcomers, and that's when he'd seen the pair of grays that the Bronsons had brought with them. He told John about how remarkably alike their coloring was to Brother Pettingill's team, and that's when the two boys hatched the brilliant idea of switching the horses on Halloween night. John's father wasn't known for socializing, but he was known for taking fastidious care of his animals. They were always clean and well groomed, whereas, according to Loyal, the Bronson team was a little worse for the wear.

John stopped Tilbet when we came to the gate that led to Bronson's farm. He dismounted, and then caught me as I slid off the sleek round back. I checked behind us and saw Loyal on the ground, holding Tub's halter.

I followed John and Tilbet as they made their way silently into the farmyard. The barn loomed large and dark in the thin moonlight. I felt a prickle of fear when John worked the door open. What if we were caught? What would I ever say to my parents? I tried to reassure myself that we weren't hurting anyone. We were just playing a prank. Yet it was a sad fact that sometimes grownups didn't understand fun. They got cranky over the simplest things. I crossed my fingers and hoped no one in the dark house beyond the paddock would wake up and look out the window to witness the shadowy gray horses moving into the barn.

Once inside, Tub and Tilbet nickered a greeting to the other horses stabled there. John led Tilbet over to one of the stalls and opened the gate. He grabbed the halter of the horse inside and pulled it out. I could just make out a large shape moving through the barn, but it was too dark to see plainly. John instructed Loyal to do the same with the other horse. Then John let Tilbet loose and gave him a slap on the rump. The horse walked obediently into the open stall door. John followed suit, pushing Tub into the enclosure next to Tilbet's.

As the boys closed the stalls, I felt a sudden pang of regret. Why had I ever thought this would be fun? What if Tilbet and Tub were afraid? What would Brother Bronson do with them when he found them in the morning?

"John?" I whispered.

"What?" he asked.

"Are you sure we should do this?"

"It's already done," he said, leading his traded horse toward the barn door. As before, I held the door open and the boys led the horses outside. The animals passed from the dim barn into the silver moonlight, their sharp hipbones casting shadows on their withers. Their coats were the same ghostly gray as the Pettingill horses, but there the resemblance ended. The Bronson horse's tails were tangled and matted with burrs. Their manes were flopping on their necks in snarled strands of dull gray. They plodded along, looking older and bonier than the horses we had brought here. We shouldn't have done this.

We didn't ride these horses. Maybe John was unfamiliar with them and didn't want to risk getting bucked off. The way they looked, I wasn't sure they'd be able to hold us up anyway.

Once we got back to John's house, it was easy to slip back into the barn and put the Bronson horses in Tub and Tilbet's stalls. I walked out the barn door with a heavy heart. The boys jostled each other and slapped one another on the back. "Good job," John said. "I'll walk you to the end of the lane, but then I've got to get inside and get some sleep so I can be up in time to see Pa's face."

"I want to see it, too," Loyal snickered. "I wouldn't miss it for the world."

"Shhhh," John said, looking back over his shoulder at the dark house as we walked out of the farmyard. "You'd have to be here by six-thirty," he said.

"Yeah, I can make it," Loyal said. "How about you, Miranda?"

"I don't know," I said. "I have chores in the morning." My conscience was twisting around inside me, making me want to jump right out of my skin. I wasn't sure I could stand watching Brother Pettingill's face when he saw what had happened to his precious team of horses. A shiver ran down my back as we walked along the dark lane that was shaded by trees and bordered by dark shrubs that could hide a myriad of imps and unseen eyes. Wary and unsettled, I followed my friends through the cold night.

"You can do those after . . ." Loyal's voice faded away, and I looked up at him. The moonlight slanting across his face painted it a deathly white. He was as still as a rock, staring down the road, his eyes wide and glistening with an eerie sheen. "I see something," he whispered hoarsely, his lips barely moving.

I had no patience for his same old spooky jokes. He couldn't scare me. "Let me guess, it's something black," I answered in a sarcastic whisper.

"No." Loyal's head barely moved as he shook it back and forth. "It's white. And big. And it's moving toward us!"

John suddenly stiffened. "I see it, too," he said, his voice tense and low. Then he gave up on any pretense of quiet. "Everybody hide!" he hollered. He ducked into the bushes at the side of the trail. With an odd little squeak, Loyal followed him into the brush.

They were going to abandon me after all, and on the pretext of seeing a ghost, no less. I squared my shoulders. I wasn't giving in to their scare tactics. Making me walk home alone was just plain mean. I planted my hands on my hips and squinted at the place where the boys had disappeared into the brush. If they didn't want me, I didn't want them, either.

I turned on my heel, ready to storm down the trail and make my way home by myself. Before I could even take one step, I caught sight of a large white figure down the lane, dancing from side to side. It didn't touch the ground. The erratic movement looked for all the world like an aggravated spirit seeking vengeance, and it was definitely headed my way.

Something grabbed the hem of my dress. I screamed in terror. John yelled, "Get down, Miranda!" He gave my skirt another hard tug. He didn't have to tell me again. I dove into the bushes, not even feeling the bare branches scratch my face until later. I didn't care. I lay flat on my stomach on the cold ground, the stones under my ribs a minor nuisance as I peered under the bush for any sign of the spook coming our way. I just knew we were being punished. We'd done wrong. Now it was too late to make things right.

Soon the stamp of impatient feet sounded on the path in front of me. I could imagine an angry spirit searching for the living prey that had been there only moments before. Of course it would find us. It was probably looking with eyes that could see in the dark. I knew it would pounce on me at any moment. My spine tingled with fear, and my stomach churned alarmingly. I pressed my cheek onto the cold earth, willing myself to disappear, my wide eyes pointed toward Loyal. I couldn't read his expression, because his face was shaded black from the shadows that hid us.

Without warning, an unearthly bellow exploded in the air. I gave a yelp of fright, then clamped my hand over my mouth and turned my face into the ground, shivering hard enough to dig myself a grave. I threw my other arm over my head, although it was poor protection from a vengeful ghost.

John moved beside me. Had it gotten him? Was it even now lifting him up in its terrible claws? Hot tears poured out of my eyes, and I caught myself whispering, "I'm sorry, I'm sorry, I'm sorry."

John jiggled me with his knee. Miraculously, he was still beside me. Whatever was after us hadn't taken him yet. I took a risk and lowered my arm just enough to see John sitting up on his knees, cautiously peering over the bushes, his face washed pale in the thin light. How could he look at that thing? He was much braver than I was. I couldn't believe my eyes when an incredulous grin slowly spread across his face. It must be a trick of the moonlight.

"John?" I asked. "What is it?"

"Come up and see," he answered. "You too, Loyal."

Slowly, I raised myself up to my knees. Just as my eyes cleared the brush, I was nearly whipped in the face. I shied back just as Loyal exclaimed, "It's old man Johnson's ornery old bull! What's wrong with him?"

The bull stamped and pawed, swinging his tail close to my face again. He let out another maddened bellow and moved off down the lane, swinging his body clumsily from side to side. My heart took its time slowing down to normal. It was only a bull. I breathed in a lungful of cold night air, willing it to stop me from trembling.

"There's a sheet caught on his horns," John explained.

Even though I drooped with relief, I was perturbed at being so badly frightened. "Who would be stupid enough to walk up to a bull and hang a sheet on his head?" I asked crossly.

John shook his head at me. "Miranda, nobody hung the sheet on the bull. He probably broke out of his pen and plowed through Sister Johnson's clothesline, snagging a sheet on his way through."

"Oh," I said.

"Let's get going," Loyal said as the bull moved out of sight into the darkness along the trail.

"I'm beat," John said. "Will you be all right without me, do you think?"

"Yeah, I think we'll survive," Loyal said. "I'll make sure Miranda gets home safely."

My heart warmed toward my two friends. "Thanks," I said. "Hey, Loyal, stop by for me in the morning, will you?"

"Sure thing," Loyal promised.

My sense of adventure spent, I wearily snuck up to my room. Settling into my own bed, comforted by the familiar contours of the mattress and pillow, I wondered if Tub and Tilbet were spending a restless night in a strange place. Were they scared? I took some comfort in knowing that at least they were together. But what would happen to them when they were discovered in the morning? I finally managed to worry myself to sleep.

I woke up to a gray morning and the sound of horse's hooves outside my room, which immediately reminded me of the horses we traded in the night. I looked out my window and saw clouds shadowing the day. A bad omen.

I slid out of bed and shivered when my feet hit the cold floor. I hurried over to the window and looked out. When Loyal spotted me, he waved his hand in wide half-circles toward himself as he sat on his horse, beckoning me to join him. I dressed and flew down the stairs and into the kitchen. My mother turned from the stove. "Where are you going in such a hurry and so early?" she asked, a frown deepening the lines on her forehead.

"Loyal needs me to help him," I said.

"So do I," Ma said. I craned my neck and looked out the window beyond her. She turned and saw Loyal throw me a restless glance, his horse prancing impatiently.

"I won't be gone long," I said.

Ma surveyed me skeptically. "Where are you going?" she asked.

"To John's," I answered. "We've got to check on something. I'll tell you all about it when I get back," I promised. "Please, Ma, may I go now? I'm usually not even up by now, so just pretend I'm still sleeping."

Ma gave up and shrugged her shoulders. Turning back toward the stove, she said, "If you take too long, I'll have your hide and John and Loyal's." She turned and pointed her wooden spoon at me. "And I'm looking forward to hearing a mighty good story when you get back."

"Thanks," I hollered, running out the door. Loyal cleared the stirrup so I could put my foot in and pull myself up behind him. I hung onto his waist as we galloped all the way to John's.

We slid to a stop in the Pettingill farmyard. Voices came from the barn. We dismounted and walked through the big double doors that we'd passed through so quietly the night before.

"My poor Tilbet!" Brother Pettingill was saying. "Oh, John, why do the spirits hate me so? And why did they take it out on my poor horses?" In the early morning light I could see Brother Pettingill pulling burrs from a gray horse's tail. "Check on Tub," he said to John. "See if he's all right."

John went into the next stall and led out another bony, matted gray horse. "Oh!" Brother Pettingill's cry was one of pain. My heart constricted with guilt when he reached over to the second horse and began trying to pull the matted mane into single strands.

Loyal moved forward. "Can I help?" he asked.

Brother Pettingill turned toward us. "I don't know if there's any help for mischief from the spirits," he intoned sorrowfully. His eyes gleamed bright with unshed tears.

"I want to help, too," I said, stepping over to the horses. "John, get me a curry comb," I said, patting the neck of the skinny gray that was supposed to be Tub.

Amidst Brother Pettingill's sorrowful exclamations, we worked at smoothing out the horse's manes and tails, then gave both of them a good brushing down. After the pair was cleaned up, Brother Pettingill was more hopeful. "John, take Tilbet and go fetch me some of that good grain from the feed store. Be quick now. With some good feed and a little bit of time, we should soon be able to restore them. Get going." Brother Pettingill turned to the imposter Tub, crooning softly in the animal's ear as he continued to work the brush over the gray coat.

John led the bony gray horse outside and climbed on its back, turning toward the feed store. The horse's gait was jerky and John sat stiffly, his tense arms holding the reins. The pretend Tilbet swished its tail saucily from side to side, proud as a housewife with a new broom.

Loyal and I followed, then pulled abreast of John. "Well, Pa was completely fooled," John said, "but I think the joke's on me. Riding this nag is giving me an awful ache. Tonight, I'm going to switch the horses back."

"I'll help," I offered.

"Will you come, too?" John asked Loyal hopefully.

"Not if I have to ride one of those horses," Loyal answered, eyeing the gray mount doubtfully.

John's eyes lit up. "Bring Miranda on your horse, then she can ride Tub back and I'll ride Tilbet."

I narrowed my eyes at John suspiciously. "Why do you get Tilbet?" I asked.

John threw his hands up and his horse shied sideways in

surprise. "You can ride Tilbet!" he exclaimed. "I don't care! Just help me switch them back!"

When I got home, I told Mama all about John and Loyal switching Brother Pettingill's and Brother Bronson's horses in the night. I somehow forgot to mention that I'd been there, too. To my surprise, Mama began to laugh. "So now what is he going to do?" she asked through an amused smile.

"He wants to switch them back tonight," I said, and then added, "He asked me to help."

Mama looked at me with her eyebrows raised. "I see. He wants to make sure his father is visited by the good spirits this time."

I shrugged. "Something like that."

"Well," she said, "better to be a good spirit than a bad one." She sent a knowing glance my way. "You may go, as long as you aren't out too late."

"Thanks, Mama!" I said.

That night after the horses were back where they belonged, I slept the sleep of the redeemed. I was late getting up the next morning, two late nights having left me exhausted. When John came around, I wasn't surprised to hear that Brother Pettingill was overjoyed at the restoration of his beloved pair of grays. I knew that Tub and Tilbet were in good hands, but I wasn't sure about Bronson's team.

It turned out that I needn't have worried about them, either. The next spring I saw a nice pair of gray horses pulling the Bronson's buggy through town with a light step, their manes and tails flowing free, their bony ridges smoothed over with well-fed muscle.

Brother Bronson sat proudly at the reins. Perhaps he had been inspired by the appearance of the two mysterious and beautiful grays, and had worked to turn his team back into those ghost horses that the spirits had surprised him with for one magical day at Halloween.

*Miranda Brady and Loyal Graham told Loyal's daughter, Donna G. Brunger, about their childhood antics on a Halloween night in 1905. They encountered a bull that had gotten loose and crashed through a clothesline, catching a sheet on his horns. One of their group traded a sad old pair of dingy gray horses for his father's well-tended and much loved team of grays. He was sorry for it the next day when his only choice was to ride one of the bony horses he had switched* (Saga of the Sanpitch, *Vol. 8 pg. 34*).

# MESSAGE FROM THE GRAVEYARD

I passed Pigeon Hollow about 10 a.m. on my way to the Manti Temple, never suspecting that the strange feeling growing in my chest was more than a mild bout of heartburn. I scooted back on the buggy seat and shifted the reins in my hands.

Perhaps it was guilt pressing down on my heart. I searched my soul for a selfish thread woven through the days I spent working at the temple. I enjoyed doing temple work, but as Bishop of Pleasant Creek, maybe I was needed back in town for some reason, and this odd feeling was a prompting telling me to turn around.

The thought swirled lazily in my head, yet I lacked the energy to pull the reins around and turn the horse. The same landscape rolled steadily past, but it looked somehow different from the countless times I'd traveled this same road. I was oddly detached from the sagebrush and scrub oak that silently watched me go by, as though I was enclosed in some sort of invisible glass bubble. I'd never felt this way before in my life. My heart beat hard and slow, and my head was light. The strange feeling crept down my arms and legs, taking over my whole body, spreading out to fill my fingers and toes. My limbs began tingling as though the circulation was being restored after having pressure on them for too long. What was happening to me?

My eyes fastened themselves to the buggy floor. Thoughts swirled languidly around in my head, circling each other without settling on anything. In the back of my mind, I felt a little prick of conscience that told me I really should watch where I was going.

It seemed a difficult task to pull my eyes away from the unremarkable spot they were gazing at on the buggy floor, but with some effort, I finally pulled my eyes up and looked at the road.

To my astonishment, a sea of faces looked back at me, a

multitude of men solemnly watching my buggy roll past. Some were dressed all in white and some were wearing dark clothes. They crowded up to the edge of the road, then spread back out over the fields, and all were staring earnestly at me.

Although I hadn't expected to see them, I wasn't afraid. In my odd state of mind, I found myself idly wondering what they were doing here.

One large man stood a little in front of the others. Although his feet weren't moving, he managed by some means unknown to me to keep pace with my buggy. The man resembled my own father, who weighed around two hundred forty pounds. The big man swept his right arm toward the gathered hordes behind him and said in a deep voice that resonated through my whole being, "These are your kindred, and we have been waiting long for the temple to be finished."

The nearer faces shifted their expressions to ones of utter yearning. My heart softened like butter on a warm windowsill at the obvious hope welling up from the depths of their souls and shining out of their eyes.

"The temple is now dedicated and accepted by our Father," the man continued. "You are our representative." My breath caught at his proclamation. I again scanned the hundreds of faces turned toward me.

The big man lowered his arm. "We want you to do for us what we cannot do for ourselves," he said. "You have heard the gospel of the Son of God. We didn't have that blessing." My eyes again roved over the vast assemblage. If all of these assembled spirits were my ancestors, where were the women? Where were the great-grandmothers? There was not one feminine face in the crowd.

I scrutinized some of the nearer faces, wondering if I had known any of these relatives in this life. None were familiar to me. How could I possibly take care of their work if I didn't even know them? Silently my heart cried, *How can I find out all their names and who they are?*

Instantly, a voice sounded in my ears, but not from the big

man. "When that will be required, it will be made known," the voice reassured me.

The pleading in the faces that were turned toward me wrenched my heart. An uncertain thought spun out of my soul, *Shall I be worthy to help them?* Tears filled my eyes as I realized I was just one man facing hundreds who were all counting on my help. A moving concern for the welfare of these souls filled my being as love for them washed over my heart. *God help me!* I cried within myself.

Facing the big man, I said in a voice broken by emotion, "God being my helper, I'll do all I can."

A deep chorus of "Amen" rumbled from the vast group of dead men, who bound me to my promise with the intensity of their eyes. Shaken to the very center of my spirit, I couldn't stop the tears from pouring down my cheeks as the collective "Amen" faded to silence. I bent my head to wipe away the tears.

After a moment I looked up again to see the road clear and the fields deserted. The Ephraim cemetery was slipping by, the headstones giving a stiff salute as the horse walked along without any urging from me. My heart burned within me, the echo of "Amen" repeating itself in my memory. The beseeching faces of my own flesh and blood who had gone on before to pave the way for me on this earth haunted every corner of my mind.

The heat within my bosom had burned up my energy as sure as a wood stove eats up kindling. Not only were my muscles as weak as a baby's, but I was tired clear through my bones. I pulled up to Sister Aagard's house in Ephraim, a place where I had occasionally taken lodging. She let me in, and I related to her my entire experience. The kindly woman fed me, after which I felt some of my strength return. When I felt I had enough energy to resume my journey, I was again on my way to the temple.

Once I got there, I sought out President Wells. With great fervor I told him of my experience on the road that morning. He listened with interest, then shook my hand warmly. "With God's help you cannot fail," he assured me.

I went about my temple ordinance work with the odd feeling

that my feet were treading on clouds. Every once in awhile, a twinge of worry would shadow my heart as I wondered how I would ever find the names for those hundreds of men who had come to me from beyond the grave seeking my help.

Toward evening, I felt a tap on my shoulder. I turned to see the temple recorder grinning at me. "Well, hello Brother Farnsworth," I greeted him. Although we shared the same surname, we hadn't as yet found a common line connecting any of our ancestors.

"Hello, Brother Farnsworth," he echoed my greeting. "I heard you had a rather unusual trip to Manti this morning."

"Yes," I said, "I'll remember it every day for the rest of my life."

Brother Farnsworth pushed his hands down into his pockets and rocked back on his heels as he surveyed me for a moment. "You know I went overseas and spent some time searching records for my family," he said. I nodded. "Well, while I was there, I found a number of Farnsworths," he said. "Unfortunately, not all of them were in my line." He put a hand up to his chin and glanced down at the floor. "Unfortunately for me, anyway." His eyes raised and bore into mine. "But for you, it may be a different story. If you'd like the records, you may have them. Can't even say why I brought them back with me, except that I felt like I should."

My heart leaped in gratitude. "Thank you!" I said. "I'd be obliged!"

The temple recorder clapped me on the back and gave a little chuckle. "They're yours," he said.

It was with warm relief but no surprise that I discovered the names I received from Brother Farnsworth matched my family line. I enlisted my daughters for help to perform work for the women who had completed their earthly sojourn before ours, but who had not bothered to meet me at the roadside asking for my help because, as a man, I couldn't do their work for them.

My faith grew as large as the impressive volume of names that my co-worker had given to me. I knew in my heart that the men who had met me on the road were in the pages and pages of information that twisted the key and unlocked the door for their eternal progression.

I never again in my life matched the feeling that immediately preceded my roadside vision, but I came close as I performed the work for my kindred dead within the walls of the temple.

*On July 16, 1888, Bishop George Farnsworth was traveling to the Manti Temple when he felt a strange sensation come over him. He raised his eyes to see a multitude of ghostly men. One who resembled his father told George that he needed to do the temple work for these dead ancestors. Bishop Farnsworth's compassionate answer was that he would do all he could with God's help. The concourses of men shouted, "Amen!" When the bishop looked up from wiping away tears, he was rolling along beside the Ephraim graveyard, and the men were gone.*

*Bishop Farnsworth told his story to temple President Daniel H. Wells, and later received genealogy records from temple recorder Frank Farnsworth that proved to be relatives of the grateful bishop, who promptly set about completing the temple ordinances for them.*

*This information is from Bishop George Farnsworth's own account, reprinted in* Saga of the Sanpitch *(Vol. 17, pg.122).*

# COLD AS DEATH

"I'm Buck Jones!" I yelled as I galloped an imaginary horse through the snow, kicking up puffs of white in my race across the yard.

"No, I'm Buck Jones," Lawrence challenged me, standing red-cheeked in his felt cowboy hat that he wore just about everywhere.

"I wanna be Buck Jones," Edgar whined, his too-big mittens hanging almost to his knees as he stood in the snow with slumped shoulders. He was probably about ready to cry. I was tempted to let him, because then I could remind him that Buck Jones never cried, so of course he couldn't be Buck Jones.

I sighed and galloped back to my friends. I knew in my head that I was really the best Buck Jones because I was already six years old. Lawrence's birthday would be next week, but today he was still five. Edgar wouldn't be six until spring. If I made them mad, though, they might go home, and I didn't want to play by myself on this fine snowy day with the promise of high adventure in every patch of untramped snow and a villain lurking behind every corner. There was no one else in sight. The world belonged to us.

"We'll take turns," I announced as I pulled my steed to a sliding stop that sprayed snow over Edgar's shoes. "I'll be Buck Jones first, then Lawrence, then Edgar."

"I wanna be first," Lawrence challenged me.

I looked him over, sizing up his determination. His jaw was clamped down and his eyes were narrowed. It looked pretty serious. Well, if I let him go first, then Edgar, then I could be last and take the longest turn. "All right," I said. "You go first. You do Buck Jones stuff, and we'll follow you. But," I said as a sudden, brilliant idea popped into my head, "if any one of us does something the other two don't dare to do, then whoever dares do it is Buck Jones forever."

Edgar's eyes went wide with awe. "Forever?" he asked.

"Forever today," I answered, confident that I would soon be the indisputable Buck Jones.

"All right," Lawrence answered, taking on the challenge. He hitched up his trousers. "Follow me, if you can." He took off running around the side of the house, whipping out his gloved finger and shooting at something behind the lilac bush that was drooping heavy with snow. The next thing I knew, his shoes slipped and he landed on his rump. He glanced back at us as we followed his tracks, Edgar whipping up his mitten to shoot the same bad guy. "He missed me," Lawrence announced loudly as he scrambled to his feet. He pointed at Edgar. "You have to dodge a bullet, same as me," he reminded him.

Edgar obediently plopped himself down in the snow, repeated, "Missed me," and stood up, ready for the next stunt.

I made a real show of it when I shot the bad guy, making rapid-fire shooting noises, then spinning in a half circle before I hit the ground. I didn't even feel the cold of the snow through the real leather gloves I'd snitched from the mudroom on my way out to play. Even though they weren't mine, they were much better at keeping out the cold than my knitted mittens. They were what Buck Jones would wear, although his wouldn't have been so big. "Missed me, you varmint!" I shouted, noticing the admiring gleam in Edgar's eyes and the glare of jealousy in Lawrence's.

Lawrence headed for the pole fence around the corral in my back yard. He climbed up to the top pole. I felt a flicker of worry. Was he going to try to walk it? Well, if he did, I would, too. I wouldn't give up being Buck Jones. Yet once Lawrence was in place, he sat on his behind and scooted along the top pole, pushing the snow off both sides as he moved along. I sneered. What was so daring about that?

Lawrence must have had the same thought, because he slid off sideways before he'd even reached the next fence post. He made a beeline for the barn. He climbed up to the hayloft, and I wondered if he was going to swing from a rope. It turned out that

Lawrence didn't come up with anything that I couldn't do.

"Edgar's turn," I announced.

"I was just getting ready to do the scariest thing," Lawrence said, swaggering around behind me to the end of the line. "You'll just have to wait until it's my turn again to see what it is," he said smugly.

Edgar's Buck Jones attempts were pitiful. He ran around with a lot of "yahoo's" and shooting at things with his baggy mitten, but the most daring thing he did was a somersault in the snow after he galloped down the barn ladder and ran outside. It was rather annoying to follow his stunt because snow dribbled down my neck. As he trotted along the edge of the ditch, I had a sudden brilliant idea.

"My turn," I said. Edgar stopped galloping and looked back at me, disappointment shadowing his eyes. It was obvious that he was perfectly happy to run around and shoot things with his finger and wasn't interested in performing any stunts of daring-do at all.

I walked to the ditch and peered over the edge. Walls of stacked rock corralled the water. The trees that stood stark and bare overhead had shaded this spot, allowing a layer of ice to form across the creek. In a patch of winter sunshine further up the ditch bank, the water was running fast between ledges of ice stuck to the rock walls. It looked just like the raging river in the last Buck Jones moving picture I'd seen in the theater.

Buck had ridden his horse off a cliff to escape the wicked desperadoes and had splashed in the water. The villains had stopped at the cliff edge and stared down at the roiling river far below, laughing evilly at the demise of the hero. Buck's horse scrambled up onto the far bank, but Buck had been underwater for so long that I was worried. What if he'd hit his head on a rock? Maybe he'd breathed in water and was really dead this time.

I scooted onto the edge of my seat and gripped the armrest, scanning the big screen for any sign of my hero. I was getting dizzy. Then I realized I was holding my breath. Just as I let out a whoosh of air, Buck's white hat appeared far down river. Underneath it was Buck Jones, dripping wet, but alive. He turned and pointed his pistol at the desperadoes. He shot four times, and four bad men went tumbling down to their deaths.

Now, seeing the swift water that disappeared underneath the ice at my feet and remembering how long Buck had been underwater, my resolve weakened. Edgar said in a small, scared voice, "Lloyd, don't go down there. It looks dangerous."

Determination settled in my chest at his words. I was looking for danger. I wanted to be Buck Jones forever. I quickly scanned the rock wall for the best way to get down. That's when I noticed a ledge of ice that had formed on the wall a few inches above the water level. I eagerly pointed at it. "Whoever can walk that ledge of ice is Buck Jones for sure," I announced, hearing the excitement in my own voice.

"Lloyd!" Edgar whined as I started picking my way down the stones. I didn't pay him any attention, but kept heading down to my self-appointed adventure. When I was on the level with the ice ledge, the rushing water was so close it sent a chill of fear through me. I glanced up at the ditch bank. Lawrence was staring down at me, his mouth slightly open, his eyebrows drawn together. Edgar was staring at me, too, his chin quivering and his eyebrows pulled up in worry. His floppy mittens were gripped together in lumpy yarn fists in front of his chest. "Lloyd!" Edgar called.

With my friends blocking my escape route, I turned away and stepped onto the ledge of ice. Slowly I put my weight on it. It held. Holding my arms out for balance, I took another small step. So far, so good. I concentrated on the end of the ledge some five feet away. Another slow step and I was beginning to feel the flush of victory. I would be Buck Jones forever. I felt like a real hero as I took yet another step.

Without any warning, the ledge gave way. My arms windmilled in helpless circles, unable to stop my body from crashing through the thin sheet of ice and into the shocking cold water below. I heard Edgar scream just before my head went under.

Desperately, I flailed my arms and caught the edge of something hard. I hung on with a death grip, the swift current tugging at my legs, coaxing them downstream. I managed to pull my head up, but the cold water seemed to have sucked the breath right out of me. It was several precious seconds before I could force my lungs to take a painful gasp of freezing cold air. My big leather gloves clamped themselves tightly on the edge of the jagged ice sheet. I was terrified. I tried to call for help, but my voice was frozen in my throat. I threw a desperate glance up at the ditch bank. My friends were nowhere in sight. Had they gone for help? Or had they figured I was a goner and run off so they wouldn't have to watch me die?

I strained to save myself, to pull my poor, numb body up onto the ice. I tried to push with my legs, to bend my knees and make them help my cold hands, but I couldn't make them work. In fact, it worried me that I couldn't even feel them. I struggled again, trying to get myself out from under the ice that both held me trapped and provided my frozen lifeline. My shallow breath grew weaker, the puffs of white whenever I exhaled growing smaller and smaller until I almost couldn't see them. I stopped struggling and stared at the big, floppy fingers of leather that gripped the ice in front of my eyes. I realized with a strangely detached sense of wonder that my own fingers didn't even seem to belong to me.

Maybe none of this was real. Maybe I was just dreaming. If I just let go, I might wake up warm and safe in my own bed, the blankets pulled up to my chin and a soft, warm pillow under my head. All I wanted was to be warm.

I was tired of holding my head up. I wanted to rest. My eyes blinked slowly. I was so tired. I relaxed my grip on the ice. It would be so easy to simply let go. With eyes half-closed, I laid my head back, the water gurgling around me soft as a feather bed. Just let go and sleep.

I was suddenly aware of someone standing above me. My eyes opened wider and I stared at a tall figure standing on the ditchbank, his hands stuck deep in his coat pockets. The man looked down at me as though I were doing something as ordinary as playing a game of marbles and he had paused to watch me shoot. He didn't appear to be angry, scared, or amused. His calm eyes captured mine and held them fast.

"Can you get yourself out?" he asked. His words snapped me awake. I knew I wasn't dreaming.

With an audience of one, the Buck Jones spirit rose in my chest. I gripped the ice with renewed energy. "Yes," I answered. The sound of my own voice gave my arms strength, and I pulled with a power beyond my own. This time I heaved myself far enough out from under the ice that I could brace myself with one knee against the broken edge and push sideways to grab the rocks with my soggy gloves. I was soon free of the frigid water, and climbed to the top of the ditch bank. I stood for a moment, confused, looking for the man. He wasn't there.

My teeth began banging together as my body was seized with shivers. I couldn't stand here wondering, I had to get home. I soon realized that walking was nearly impossible. My pant legs were iced over and unbending. I had to make my way stiff-legged. When I reached my house, I tried to open the door, but the gloves on my hands had twisted themselves into claws of frosted brown leather and were useless for gripping the doorknob. I panicked. Would I escape drowning only to freeze to death while standing on my very own porch?

"Ma!" I cried, swinging one leg back like a log, bringing it forward in a roundhouse kick to the wooden door. "Ma!" I called again. The tears that began rolling down my face felt hot against the cold flesh of my cheeks. I swung another awkward kick at the door.

It opened, and my mother's eyes went from narrowed annoyance to wide surprise. "Lloyd!" she exclaimed as she grabbed my shoulder and pulled me into the house, nearly knocking me off balance when she moved me faster than my stiff limbs could follow. Only her grip on my coat kept me from falling on my face. "What on earth happened to you?" she asked as she began to free me from my tomb of clothing.

"I fell in the ditch," I said, the tears flowing even faster now that I was safe in my warm house and in my mother's care.

Ma was a blur of activity as she wrestled me out of my frozen clothes and rubbed me down with a dry towel. She wrapped me in a blanket and carried me into the kitchen, never mind that I was too big to be carried. She sat me down in a chair by the stove and opened the oven door. Dry heat surged out, embracing me in warmth. Ma grabbed my feet in her hands and began to rub vigorously.

"How did you get out?" she asked, looking up at me with worried eyes.

"I tried to pull myself out, but it was too hard." I sniffed and wiped my nose with the back of my hand, which was prickling with pain as it thawed out. "Then a man came and asked if I needed help."

"What man?"

I shook my head. "I don't know who he was, but he looked nice. I mean, friendly. He didn't seem worried about me, so I quit feeling afraid. Then I could get out."

"Didn't you ask him his name?"

"By the time I climbed up to the ditch bank, he was gone," I said.

Ma shook her head. "He didn't wait to see you safely home?"

"No, he just disappeared," I said.

"Well, of all the nerve," Ma said angrily.

I shrunk inside myself. "Please don't be mad, Ma," I begged.

Ma pulled me into a crushing hug. "I'm not mad at you," she assured me. She began rubbing my calves. My feet were burning from the circulating blood warming them back to life. I made a pained face.

"I'll go make you some hot chocolate," Ma said.

When I was finally warm and dry, Ma said, "Lloyd, I want you to show me where you fell in the creek."

"Right now?"

"Yes, right now," Ma said, wrapping a scarf around my neck.

We walked back to the ditch bank without seeing another person. I pointed down to the broken sheet of ice.

"There," I said.

"Oh, Lloyd," Ma said softly. Her hand on my shoulder gripped tighter. After a moment, she asked, "Where was the man standing?"

I pointed to a spot beside us. "Right there."

Ma looked down at the ground. "Are you sure?" she asked.

"Yes," I said. "He stood there and looked at me and asked me if I could get myself out, just like I said."

Ma bent down and scanned the snow with her eyes. "What's wrong?" I asked.

"There are no footprints."

"Yes there are!" I said, pointing at the dents in the snow made by our feet. I could even see where Edgar and Lawrence had stood, and the scuffed snow from where they'd run away.

"There are no man-sized footprints," Ma said as she straightened up.

I stared at the ground in disbelief. She was right. A violent shiver suddenly shook me from head to foot. "Come on, Lloyd, you're getting chilled," Ma said. I let her lead me home.

That Saturday, the moving picture show playing at the theater was Buck Jones. I stayed home.

*Somewhere in the early 1900s, Lloyd H. Parry remembers finding himself in a deadly predicament when he took a dare to walk a narrow ice ledge in the frozen ditch so that he could be dubbed "Buck Jones," a daring-do hero of silent films.*

*When the ledge broke, Lloyd managed to catch the edge of the ice that sheeted over the water. His young friends were so frightened, they abandoned him. Struggling didn't seem to help any. Unsure of how to get out of his predicament, Lloyd threw a desperate glance up to the ditch bank and saw a friendly-faced stranger looking down at him. "Can you get yourself out?" the man asked.*

*Taking courage from the man's presence, Lloyd answered,*

*"Yes!" He managed to pull himself out of the water and onto the bank. He looked for the stranger, but the man was gone.*

*With clothes frozen stiff, Lloyd had to kick the door to let his mother know he was there. When asked about the stranger, Lloyd couldn't identify him, and the man was never seen again* (Saga of the Sanpitch, *Vol. 24, pg. 82).*

# THE HIDEOUT

I stared gloomily at the dark cave entrance. My jail cell. I was separated from my family just as surely as if there were bars between us.

I turned and drank in the valley with my eyes. It appeared deceptively peaceful, with warm rays of the setting sun coloring it golden. I wanted to go down there in the worst way, yet I knew that what looked so inviting was actually a giant trap, with the bait being my very own home and family.

My eyes roved hungrily over the landscape, settling at last on the tiny town of Freedom where my three wives lived with my children. Freedom. How ironic. It had seemed the perfect name when my brother and I had founded it. Yet if I were in Freedom right now, my freedom would surely be taken from me. I would be bound and carried off to jail.

My hands curled into fists. What right did the government have to send officers to Utah Territory to enforce a law against plural marriage when we weren't even part of the United States? The truth was, they had no right. I should stand up to them, challenge their authority. My chin thrust out, and I took several rapid steps toward town before a sobering thought penetrated my anger. What help would I be to my family in jail? Right now I was away from them, but I wasn't locked up. I still had some freedom.

I stopped walking and kicked at a rock, sending it skittering into a clump of sagebrush. As much as it galled me, it was better for my family that I stay in hiding until the United States marshals left the valley. This was the devil's work, plain and simple, and I had to trust in God to help me fight this enemy.

I walked back to my hideout and ducked inside the dark cave. The entrance was narrow and cleverly concealed behind a crease in the rock. That I'd ever found it at all was a miracle in itself.

I said my prayers, feeling as though the pleadings I sent up to heaven could not penetrate the ceiling of rock that kept them from reaching divine ears. I curled up into my sorry little bedroll and gave in to worry. Was my brother Parley looking out for my family? He had his own wife and children to take care of, but since he only had one wife, he wasn't in danger of arrest.

A picture flashed into my mind of Parley sitting at his table, finishing off his supper. My imagination brought up his wife, Effie, carrying in a warm apple pie and setting it in front of Parley with a tender smile. As I was particular to apple pie, this thought made my stomach rumble and my mouth water. How cruel was fate. Here I was, forced to eat cold, dry food because a fire might alert the marshals. I slept on the ground, alone in my forced solitude without even a horse to keep me company.

I turned over on my hard bed of dirt and tried to settle my head more comfortably on the folded blanket that served as my pillow. Parley would watch out for my family. He'd proven to be dependable from the time we'd first claimed the land Freedom was built upon. Bishop Irons had taken exception to my building a log house on the property, even though he had no legal claim to it. When I refused to tear down my home, the bishop declared his intention to file on it. Well, that had been my intent, too, and his announcement spurred me to action. I sent Parley on a good horse to Salt Lake City to file the necessary papers for us and some of the other members of the Draper family to get Freedom in our name. My younger brother proved his mettle, covering the distance to the capital in one day. Upon his triumphant return, he gleefully told me that he had passed the bishop and his assistant riding north for the same purpose that he had just accomplished.

"When he saw me, Doc, his face turned purple!" Parley grinned, using my family nickname and delighted at the memory of his achievement. "We won!"

I nodded in satisfaction. It seemed right that we had title to the land that we'd already cleared, cultivated, and planted.

Bishop Irons was livid. He enlisted my father by some means

of persuasion, perhaps the threat of church reprimand or eternal torment, to agree to join in his campaign to get me to relinquish the land. When I saw the carriage with my father and the bishop's assistant pull up to my cabin, I stepped out to greet them with a rifle in my hands. Pa's eyes widened. The assistant paled. "We're here on assignment from Bishop Irons," the assistant called out in a falsely brave voice. I shifted the gun on my arm and the assistant ducked behind my father. "You must give this land back for the betterment of the church," he squeaked from the safety of Pa's shadow.

"The betterment of the church or the bishop?" I asked, not bothering to keep the sarcasm out of my voice. "I only have business with my father. No one else. Come on, Pa," I urged, swinging my gun barrel off to the side. My father slowly raised himself off the buggy seat, then stepped down to the ground. As he made his way toward me, I pointed the gun past him at the bishop's assistant. "Now go back home and tell Bishop Irons that it's all taken care of. My family stays here," I said. Without another word, the assistant shook the reins across the back of the horse. The horse took off at a trot, leaving us in a cloud of dust.

I smiled a hard little smile as I thought that for all I knew, it had been Bishop Irons who had summoned the United States Marshals here for the sole purpose of getting even with me. I rolled over onto my back and stared up into the darkness. This way of thinking was getting me no rest at all. I had to change my thoughts. I turned them toward home, where I imagined my wives settling the little ones into their beds. In my mind, I heard little Wilmont say, "I've got the bestest Daddy of anyone!"

Then Fanny bent over our little son. "Yes, you do," and she kissed him. Wearing a smile of paternal pride, I finally drifted off to sleep.

The galloping of horse's hooves jarred me awake, jerking me upright as fear of discovery stabbed my heart. I stared wildly at the entrance to my hideout where a faint gray light showed early dawn. I cocked my head, listening desperately past my frantic breathing, trying to find the source of the thundering hoofbeats. My head slowly tipped up as my ears followed the sound of mad galloping. It was coming from the hill that formed the ceiling of the cave over my head.

Someone was hunting me. They couldn't have known that they were riding directly over my hideout, moving so fast that if they didn't slow down they might break their necks, or their horses'. It would be a pity to lose good horses. It sounded like a whole army, galloping hard, moving off the mountain toward town. How could the army spare so many horses and men to look for one polygamist? And why were they were moving down from the mountain? Had they spent the night up there? Why? I would have thought they'd be heading up at the first light of day to look for me instead of returning in the pre-dawn grayness.

Gradually the galloping hooves faded away to nothing. All I could hear was my own ragged breathing. The air was strangely still. Not even the usual songbirds sounded a good morning call to the world. Even after my breathing calmed, the dead silence hung eerily over my hideout. My skin crawled cold and prickly along my shoulders. I tried to shrug it off, but something strange charged the air with silent expectation.

Unable to sit still one moment longer, I crept to the entrance of the cave, listening intently. Cautious as a hunted rabbit in its burrow, I slowly poked my head out. I didn't see anyone, or anything.

I crawled outside and stood, hugging the rock wall to my back in case I needed to duck back inside. I scanned the valley, but saw neither head nor tail of horses or riders. There wasn't even the smell of dust kicked up by pounding hooves. Impossible. That many horses would have kicked up a suffocating cloud of dust.

With mounting apprehension, I climbed up the slope to the top of the hill that served as the roof of my primitive home. The sky was steadily lightening. I stared at the undisturbed hilltop. I was chilled that my careful scrutiny revealed no sign of any passing horses. I watched as the sun worked its way closer to the mountaintops, gradually lighting the hill and proving to my reluctant eyes that the ground was completely undisturbed. There was no loosened soil, no hoof marks on the ground, no spoor at all. The hair at the nape of my neck prickled. It was impossible that the ground spread flat before me would be devoid of any tracks. Even if I had been mistaken about the hooves belonging to horses, there had been a great many of some kind of animal galloping across the hill over my head. I knew I hadn't been dreaming. The hoofbeats had woken me.

I grabbed my elbows with my hands and rubbed up and down on my arms. I didn't expect it to do any good. The chills I felt weren't from the cold morning air.

I backed down the hill, glancing up the mountainside from where the mysterious travelers must have come. I made it back to the cave entrance as the sun burst forth from behind its mountain bed, stretching its rays across the valley in an early morning exercise.

I started with alarm when the new light picked out two horses making their way up the foothills toward me. The lead horse had a rider, but he was too far away for me to make out who it was.

I instantly froze in place, using a lesson learned from wild animals that held still to blend in to the landscape and avoid detection from the enemy. I studied the lone rider for several minutes before I swept a wary, appraising glance across the valley. It appeared that the rider was alone. As far as I could tell, he wasn't wearing an army uniform. Still, this could be a trick.

I slipped inside the cave, fairly certain that I was as yet undetected. Once inside, I lay on my belly and stuck my head out of the opening. Whoever was coming wouldn't be looking for a face at ground level. As the rider drew closer, an assurance that there was something familiar about him grew stronger.

"Pa!" the voice carried faintly to my ears like the sound of heavenly trumpets. I stood and hurried down the slope. My son Joe's face lit up when he caught sight of me. He corrected his course to come straight on. "Pa, the marshals are gone," he called, his eyes alive with excitement.

My mouth fell open in amazement. "Why? When?"

"Just this morning," Joe answered. "They up and left, real sudden-like. Hadn't said a thing yesterday about moving camp today."

I stared at Joe, joy overtaking my heart. I was free again.

But what had happened to send the soldiers away? Perhaps the ghostly horse brigade had been visible after all. If the marshals had seen a mounted army galloping down from the mountain, it could have been enough to make them turn tail and run. I would have liked to have seen it myself. Had they been sent just to clear the way for a lonely man to return home?

"Well, son, if the pigpen's cleaned out, I'm ready to go," I said. Joe grinned at me as I swung up into the saddle of the spare mount he'd brought with him. We turned and headed down the slope, making a beeline for home and Freedom.

*William "Doc" Draper's great granddaughters LaWanna Peterson and Carolyn Bessey told the author about Parley Draper's race to file on the town of Freedom for the Draper family after the local bishop demanded that they abandon their cabins so that the bishop himself could file on the parcel.*

*On his way to Salt Lake City, the bishop realized his plan had been thwarted when he passed Parley on the trail riding back from filing legal claim to the land. The bishop enlisted the help of Doc and Parley's father, but Doc rescued his aging father from the bishop's assistant at gunpoint.*

*In the early 1880s when U.S. Marshals came to Utah Territory looking for polygamists, Doc Draper hid in a cave in the mountains west of Freedom. While in the cave, he heard the distinct sound of horse hooves galloping over the hill above his head. Summoning the courage to investigate, he found no tracks or traces of any animals.*

*Carolyn remembers that about a hundred years later, her father Mayo Sorensen flew over the west mountain in an airplane in an attempt to locate his grandfather's hideout. He dropped a roll of toilet paper to mark the spot where he saw the cave from the air, but couldn't find it again when he returned for a ground search.*

*LaWanna remembers the story differently, that Mayo actually did find the cave and spent some time inside after which he reported that he had also heard the ghostly hoofbeats.*

# NINE LIVES

Mama stormed into the room and slammed the door behind her. I looked up from the table in alarm, my teeth tearing through the thick slice of homemade bread and honey that I had just put into my mouth. Mama looked so near to breaking into tears, I hardly noticed the veneer of golden sweet honey stuck to my chin. A line of worry was stamped between Mama's eyes, blazing out above cheeks stained hot pink.

"What's the matter?" I asked through my bite of sweet bread.

Mama didn't even remind me not to talk with my mouth full, so I knew something was weighing heavily on her mind. "It's Tom," she said.

I set my slice of bread down on a plate, wiped my chin with the back of my hand, and said, "Again?" I couldn't figure out why she was so upset over yet another complaint about our big tomcat. It was becoming a habit for the neighbors to reproach us for our black cat and his noisy forays into the night when he serenaded the lady cats.

Mama pulled a chair out across the table from me and sank down into it as I swallowed my mouthful. "I can't take any more of it, Eardley, I really can't," she said. Her eyes filled with tears. "It's not just the neighbors complaining about Tom's cater-wauling." She spread her hands. "It's all these kittens around the place. It's hard enough to feed the two of us without all these cats."

I looked Mama straight in the eye. "They can't all be Tom's fault," I said in his defense.

Mama covered her eyes briefly with one hand. My shoulders tensed as I wondered if I'd spoken out of turn. I didn't mean for my remarks to come across as disrespectful. Then I saw what might have been a smile tugging at the corner of her mouth, and I relaxed.

Mama moved her hand from her eyes and reached out to

cover my fingers. "Son," she said, wiping at her eyes with her other hand, "I know you're fond of that old tomcat, but it's not fair to the neighbors to have him out there squalling at all hours of the night. They have a right to their sleep. They've all got work to do in the day."

I stared down at the golden glaze soaking into the bread on my plate and realized I wasn't hungry anymore. It's not even like I babied that old Tom. He wouldn't have stood any babying, anyway. He was a self-reliant cat, submitting to a pat on the head if he felt like it, but never begging for attention. He'd sit on the porch for his milk just because he knew he had a right to it. Sometimes he would wind his way around me, his dark tail curling around my calf as he slid slowly through my legs, but only if it suited his purpose.

Tom wasn't really that old, either, only five or six years. We just called him Old Tom. I liked his independence. He made me feel better somehow, what with Pa dead and all. It seemed that if a cat could make it in this world on his own, not caring what others thought of him, then I could make it, too.

There were even times when I wished I could be in his skin. Sometimes when I was crossing a field by the creek or creeping home soft and silent after dusk, I pretended I was Tom, going wherever I wanted to go, life choices made by something as simple as a scent on the wind. I understood that cat, and I liked to imagine that he had similar feelings for me.

"Brother Inkley said that if I don't do something about it, he's going to shoot Tom."

My heart leapt in alarm at her words, but my voice came out calm. "Let him." I shrugged as if I didn't care. I'd much rather have Old Tom's blood on someone else's hands. Besides, Brother Inkley would probably miss.

Mama must have been thinking along the same lines, but with a different conclusion. "Eardley, if people start shooting their guns off in the dark, they might hit something, or someone, besides Tom." I was quiet. I hadn't thought of that. "And if they did somehow manage to shoot Tom, they might just wound him.

He could crawl away and hide, bleeding and suffering for days before he finally dies. I don't want that for him."

The lump in my throat sat hard and cold as I thought of Tom lying helpless with a shattered bone in his leg or gutshot and mewing piteously in agony. When I didn't say anything, Mama continued, "It's not fair for us to expect others to solve the problem for us." She fell silent and watched me. What was I supposed to say? "Eard, I need your help on this," Mama said.

Reluctantly, I looked up at her. The pink spots on her cheeks had faded, leaving her pale and so tired looking that the shadows under her eyes mirrored the night sky that served as Tom's theater. I suddenly realized with a catch in my heart that Mama was more important to me than any old cat. I didn't want anything to happen to her, even though I was a nearly grown man of twelve.

"All right," I said, my heart so heavy it sank down into my stomach.

"Do you want to finish eating first?" Mama asked.

I only shook my head.

Mama pulled out our round, galvanized washtub. Slowly I pushed myself up from the table and opened the door for her. She carried the tub outside and set it down underneath the water pump. "Go find Tom," Mama said as she began to work the pump handle.

Dragging my feet, I headed for the barn. Since it was afternoon, I was willing to bet that Tom would be relaxing and resting up for his nightly prowl. "Stupid cat," I said out loud as I pushed open the barn door.

As if answering to his name, Tom lifted his head and peered at me through eyes narrowed into contented slits of yellow. I strode over to him and scooped him up. Surprised at the suddenness of finding his feet off the floor, Tom pushed his forelegs against me and his claws found the skin beneath my shirt. I welcomed the sharp, needley pain in my shoulder, hoping he was drawing blood. It seemed more humane to give

Tom the semblance of a fighting chance, even if he really had none.

By the time I had walked back to the yard, Mama had the washtub overflowing with water. She held a gunny sack in her hands. When she saw me coming, she opened the neck of the sack like the mouth of some flabby, eyeless beast, hanging skinny and starving from her fingers. Mama's face was solemn. I lifted the scrabbling Tom toward the sack.

Tom's eyes were wide open, his head turning this way and that as he tried to figure out what was going on. I positioned him over the opening, his ears flattened against his head. I dropped him suddenly, his claw snagging my sleeve as he yowled in surprise.

The claw yanked free, the sudden weight of the cat making Mama's arms drop. She quickly squeezed the neck of the sack closed before handing me a piece of twine, which I twisted around the fabric she had bunched in her hands. I tied a knot, trying to ignore the yowls of protest coming from the surging sides of burlap as Tom fought to find a way out. After a quick and anguished glance at me, Mama lifted the sack and plunged it into the water.

The screech that came from the sack was enough to freeze the blood in my veins. The gunnysack became a blur of explosive energy, kicking water out a good six feet into the air as it writhed and squealed and scrabbled in frenzy. Mama looked as though she'd been butted in the backside by a bull with sharp horns. Her horrified expression was more than I could stand. I hauled the furious bundle of dripping burlap out of the water, getting as wet as I ever had in a downpour, and I quickly untied the string. Tom was out of the sack before I could even tip it sideways. He streaked across the grass, his lean body showing every push of his frantic legs as the fur plastered itself wetly to his sides.

"Oh, Eard," Mama said, her face dripping from splashed water mixed with her tears. "Now we'll have to start all over."

"Do we still have to do it?" I asked.

Mama stood quiet for a minute, looking after Tom, who'd

disappeared behind the barn like a wanted criminal. "I'm afraid so. We've got to take care of our responsibility," Mama said. "Think of it this way. If someone's cow raided our garden, stomping holes and eating our vegetables, we'd be pretty upset." I didn't answer. There was no way she could convince me that Tom did as much damage as a cow.

Mama sighed. "Tom is robbing our neighbors of sleep just as surely as a loose cow would rob us of our food. We have to take care of it." Out of the corners of my eyes, I could see Mama looking me over before she said, "But not today. Maybe Tom won't even feel like going out tonight. Come on, Eardley, let's go inside." Mama put her arm around my shoulders, and I let her.

A week passed before Mama pulled the washtub out onto the lawn again. I knew that explaining to the neighbors that she had tried to get rid of the tomcat had done nothing to satisfy them and their idea of justice. She would just have to try again, and get it right this time.

With grim determination, Mama worked the old pump handle. Beside the metal tub was an old cast iron stove top, big enough to completely cover the washtub. I was sent to find Tom again, but as I suspected, he didn't trust me. I used a piece of bacon to lure him close enough to throw a towel over him. There was still a fight before I gathered him up into my arms, towel and all. His screeches of protest were loud enough to make my ears ring. Tom fought against his bonds like a madman.

This time I dumped the cat and towel into the sack together, and Mama heaved him into the washtub without pause. As the water exploded out of the tub from Tom's frantic churning, Mama and I each lifted an end of the stove top and set it down on the turbulent water. I could feel the ground shaking under my feet as Tom fought in vain to escape. The time we waited for Tom's struggles to cease was agonizing. Every thud punched another hole in my heart. I was trembling, shot through with such guilt and pain that it was difficult to stand up straight. I wanted to curl up and be sick to my stomach, but Mama needed me, so I swallowed the bile and waited. Eventually the thrashing subsided, the desperate thumps faded away to silence, and all was still.

Mama walked slowly toward the house, her shoulders rounded with dejection. My throat hurt. I turned and made my way to the apple orchard. Underneath one of the trees I found a spot soft enough to shovel out a cat-sized hole. When I was through with my solemn task, I leaned the shovel against the tree and walked back to the yard. I lifted up one end of the heavy stove top and let it slide from off the washtub, not even caring that it scarred the yard when the edge thudded deep into the ground. Then it tipped heavily onto its top and lay still.

With a leaden heart, I picked up the top of the sack that floated hopelessly on the water and lifted it out. It ran a small river of tears over the edge of the tub and onto the ground. I held it out away from me and made my solo funeral procession to the base of the apple tree. I set the sack down and untied the knot, working at the wet twine until my fingers were sore, glad that I was feeling pain for the sake of Old Tom. When the neck was free, I upended the bag over the hole. Tom's limp body poured out into the earth. Clods of dirt rolled down the sides of the grave and clung to his sodden fur. He looked like a dirty old rag carelessly discarded without a second thought. Poor Old Tom, hated just for being himself. He hadn't meant to bother anyone. I should have tried to explain to the neighbors, gone door to door in Tom's defense. Now it was too late.

I grabbed up my shovel and erased the sight of my dead cat with shovel after shovel of dirt, hurrying to finish, my movements haphazard in their madness, trying to get done before my eyes filled with too many tears to see.

My heart-rending task complete, I shouldered my shovel and walked back, eyes following my feet dragging across the yard. I tried to forget the haunting memory of a soggy black cat lying still and dead at the bottom of a lonely grave.

Neither Mama nor I talked much that evening. I went to bed early without a fuss. I tossed and turned for a long time, fighting the wakefulness that stuck stubbornly to my uneasy memories.

When sleep finally came, it was sporadic and troubled. I dreamt of Tom and his fierce struggle to survive, the way he fought to breathe air instead of the suffocating water that was all his lungs could find. I woke up suddenly, my heart racing in a panic of choking on water.

A haunting meow sounded through the house so softly I had to question if it was left over from my dream. My eyes darted to the window where gray light of early dawn was peering in through the glass. The faint meow sounded again, weak and eerily familiar. A flash of unease darted into my chest. Would I be haunted by nightmares for the rest of my life because I helped murder my cat?

"Eardley!" Mama called, her voice quick and excited. I threw off the covers and ran for the kitchen. Mama stood by the open door. I glanced out through the screen and skidded to a stop. There, sitting on the porch, was a damp black cat, his eyes caked with dirt and his coat streaked with mud. I couldn't believe it. After all we'd done to him, twice even, Old Tom had come home begging for help.

"Tom!" I said in a voice that surprised me with a sob. I opened the screen door and picked up my cat. He didn't resist, but hung heavy in my arms. I sat at the kitchen table, and Mama dampened a cloth before gently wiping Tom's eyes clean. He tried to twist his head away, but was so weak that his legs barely moved as Mama finished her task.

I petted Tom's head, even though it was crusted with mud. I carefully picked out small bits of dirt as my fingers ran lightly between his ears and down his back. My eyes stung when I imagined what the poor cat must have suffered. First drowning, then having to dig himself out of his grave.

Eyes swimming with tears, Mama set a saucer down on the table beside me. Tom turned his head when he caught the scent of milk. Instead of putting him on the floor, I leaned over so he could get to the milk while still in my arms. He lapped weakly for a minute or two, then collapsed back into my lap so suddenly that I wondered if he was really dead at last. Anxiously scanning his body, I noticed tiny dirt clods on his chest fur rising and falling rhythmically.

Mama made a little nest of blankets next to the stove, and I lowered Tom onto them. We looked at each other over the weary cat's head. It was as though I could read Mama's thoughts. The next time Tom passed over beyond the grave would be of a time appointed by a power higher than me or even Mama.

And that's what we told the neighbors. Tom obviously wasn't done living yet and had come back from the grave to prove it.

*Eardley Burdett Madsen tells of the time in the early 1900s when his widowed mother, overrun with litters of kittens and harassed by complaints from the neighbors over the nightly caterwauling from their tom cat, finally decided she had to kill the cat. The first effort at drowning failed, but the second succeeded, even to the point of a sad burial of the water-logged body in a little grave dug by Eardley himself. Unbelievably, the next morning Tom was scratching at the door, muddy and mewing. He was quickly treated to a gentle cleaning and a bowl of warm milk. No other attempt was ever made to hasten him into the next life (Saga of the Sanpitch, Vol. 14, pg. 52).*

# VISITORS

Stabbing my broom under the benches with quick jabs, I made certain that every errant wood shaving was swept up. After eleven years in the making, the Manti Temple was finally completed, and it was up to me as janitor to make sure that it was clean and ready for the dedication ceremony. As I worked, I ran through a mental checklist of things I still had to finish with only two days left to do them. It would take a miracle to get everything ready.

My thoughts were jarred from their path by a sudden burst of wind that struck so hard it shook the windowpanes. I straightened and threw a worried glance at the polished glass. Clouds scudded across the darkening sky, hurrying toward some cosmic appointment. Another strong wind rattled the window.

I frowned. Even though I didn't want it to be stormy for the dedication ceremony, that wasn't what was nagging at the back of my mind. There was something else that was very important. What was it? I racked my brain. Something about the glass was making me uneasy.

Suddenly remembering, I threw my broom aside and dashed for the stairs, jumping down them two at a time. What had seemed like a good idea this morning might now cause me hours of extra work. I had thought that opening the windows to the fresh spring air after scrubbing the rooms would help drive out the smell of turpentine. Now this sudden, unexpected wind would be blowing dirt into those newly cleaned rooms, setting me back further off my schedule. I had to get those windows shut, and fast!

Bursting through the doorway into the first room, I was startled to see the back of a man in a dark suit standing in the center. He didn't turn around to look at me, even though my entrance was anything but quiet. He began to walk slowly along the length of the room with his hands clasped behind his back, studying the walls and furnishings.

I didn't take the time to address him. I hurried to the first window, a blast of mischievous spring air throwing the long draperies at me. I wrestled with the fabric until I could finally snap the window shut.

As I moved to the next open window, the stranger continued his unhurried way through the room. He still didn't look my way. I had conducted several tours for curious visitors over the past few days, and I figured that this man was here for the same reason. As soon as I was through, I'd have to tell him that he wasn't supposed to be in here without a guide. For now, I had a more pressing problem at hand than a benign trespasser.

I will admit that I was a little put out when he didn't bother to acknowledge me. If he had looked behind him, he would see the predicament I was in and might offer me a hand. Yet he seemed oblivious to me, caught up in his inspection of the building. Well, I reasoned, closing the windows wasn't his job. It was mine.

When I finished pulling the last window shut, I turned and saw that the man was gone. I hurried into the next room and there he was, walking slowly across the carpet, looking around with as much interest as before. I quickly shut the blustering wind behind walls of glass. There. I was done.

Relieved of my urgent task, I turned to address the stranger and saw him disappearing through the doorway leading to the next room. I hurried after him. "Sir?" I said. When I reached the doorway I stopped. The room was empty. That was strange. Where could he have gone? The only place the visitor could possibly be was underneath the benches. Yet why would anyone hide in the temple? Maybe he was up to no good. Cautiously, I bent over and peered underneath the row of white benches. The floor was clear.

I straightened and looked uncertainly at the single door set in the side wall. It was supposed to be locked. Had I forgotten? I hurried over and twisted the knob. The door didn't budge. I had locked it. I couldn't even go through it myself because I didn't have my keys with me. Then where had the man gone? I knew he hadn't walked past me, and this locked door was the only other way out of this windowless room.

My thoughts battled in my head as I double-checked every corner and any possible place of concealment. He simply wasn't there. A chill crept across my shoulders and ran down my arms, making the hair stand on end. Who had I been following through the temple? It couldn't have been anyone of this earth.

With frequent glances over my shoulder, I made my way back up the stairs. I quickly put the broom away and retired for the night in the small room within the temple walls that had been assigned to me as caretaker.

The next couple of days all but drove the single visitor from my mind. Hoards of people came to Temple Hill in buggies and on horseback. Whole families were camping out around the base of the hill so they could hear the dedicatory service, which turned out to be a service to remember. Many said they could hear angels singing, even after the choir had stopped. The church authorities from Salt Lake City shook my hand and congratulated me on the fine condition of the building.

On the last evening, I was elated but exhausted. Along with high emotions, I had been running from station to station to make sure everything was in order. Now that it was all over and everyone had gone back to their homes or their campfires, all I could think of was falling into bed.

A sudden flash pulled my eyes to the window. Then a rumble sounded, as low and insistent as a hunger pang. A thunderstorm was brewing. Out of habit, my mind darted around the building, searching for anything that might not be secured. Were all the doors fastened? Were all the windows closed? I thought so, but when the rain smacked against the window like little beads of glass that broke and leaked down the pane, I could not convince myself that all the sealing room windows were secured. The afternoon had been sunny and warm, and all the bodies packed inside the temple for the dedication had made it rather hot and stuffy. I couldn't be sure that all the windows had been shut after people left, and I knew I wouldn't be able to sleep if I didn't check.

I made my way down the stairs. *Why do I have to have such a noisy conscience?* I wondered grumpily. I yawned as I reached out to open the door of the first sealing room. I twisted the knob and pushed the door in. What I saw jolted me as swift as a lighting bolt, and I stood frozen in the doorway. My feet refused to take me into the room, into the presence of an angel hovering in the air over the altar. The angel's clothes and skin were glowing with such brilliant white light that it filled every corner of the room with a brightness whiter than the full noon sun.

In spite of the peaceful countenance on the heavenly face, my legs trembled. Of its own accord, my hand jerked the door closed, and I ran. A frightened sob escaped my throat as I flew up the stairs, not even touching half of them in my haste. When I reached my room, I slammed the door behind me and fell to my knees. A desperate plea rose from the depths of my terrified soul up to heaven, begging Father to take away the unreasonable fear that had my heart squeezed in its cruel grip. As I pled for deliverance, the trembling in my limbs steadied, and my heart calmed, washed over with a peace that spread throughout my body. Assured that the sacred building was in good hands, I rolled over onto my humble bed and relaxed into a deep and comforted sleep.

The next day was washed clean and smelled new, promising growth for the crops planted in the fields spread out around the foot of Temple Hill. I found President Daniel Wells and confided to him that I had seen an angel. He smiled warmly. Clapping me on the shoulder, he leaned in close and said through his long, white beard, "Brother Alstrom, without a doubt there are angels in attendance here, but it is not given to everyone to see them." His blue eyes were full of kindness and his words filled my heart with reassurance. He nodded at me and gave my shoulder a friendly squeeze before walking away.

I stood for a moment, looking around at the building I had been given the charge of keeping clean and secure. "All right, all you angels," I said. "Just remember, if you open it, close it, and we'll get along just fine."

*Young Women's Journal published in April of 1890 carries the original account of Peter Alstrom's experiences in Vol. 1, pages 213-215. As the first caretaker of the Manti Temple, Alstrom was cleaning for the dedication ceremony when a fierce windstorm struck. Hurrying to close windows, he saw a man in a dark suit glancing curiously at the walls and furnishings. The janitor wasn't alarmed at this unexpected visitor.*

*When Alstrom finished his task and turned to address the man, he was startled to find himself alone. The room was locked, and there was no other way the man could have left without passing the puzzled janitor.*

*The night following the dedication ceremony was dark and stormy. Alstrom was preparing to retire for the night when he remembered an open window in a sealing room. Opening the door to the room, he saw a brilliant white personage standing over the altar. He forgot all about the window and ran upstairs, where he prayed to have his foolish fear taken away. He was instantly calmed.*

*The next morning, President Wells assured Peter that there was nothing to fear from an angel of the Lord. Doubtless there were angels in the temple, but not everyone was given the ability to see them.*

# GO HOME

My back and arms begged me to stop, yet I fed another log into the saw blade. After two days of sawing wood, the action was branded into my muscles. When the other brethren had been here with me, the work went faster, but I didn't blame them for going home after all the corral posts were cut. That's what we'd come for. It was my own personal project that kept me here alone.

I stood up and wiped the sweat out of my eyes with my handkerchief, then stared at the grimy piece of once-white fabric. I let out a humorless snort. My Mary would have snatched that dirty handkerchief away quick as a mouse if she'd been there to see it. I missed my wife, even if she was a bit fussy about dirt, a full time worry in this wilderness. She was a loving mother to our little son and brand-new baby daughter. I had never regretted marrying her in any of the five years that she had shared my name.

I hunched my shoulders and stretched my arms forward, pointing my calloused fingers toward the window of the sawmill, pulling my poor, over-worked muscles into a long stretch. I would be glad when I could leave for home and Mary's good cooking. I was mighty tired of hard bread and dried meat.

I helped myself to a long drink of water. The extra day or two of cutting wood would pay off in the long run when I finished enough for a fence to keep the rabbits and deer from making a feast of our ripening garden.

With thoughts of Mary in my head, I bent again to my solo task. The thought of my cozy, warm home with my wife and two children, little Hazard and baby Sarah, and the heavenly smells I imagined coming from the kitchen filled with Mary's cooking lifted my spirits and put renewed energy into my efforts.

"Go home," someone said. I stood quickly and turned to see who had come in behind me. Perhaps one of the brethren had returned to give me a hand. I scanned the room, then frowned. It was empty, yet the voice had sounded so near. Puzzled, I walked to the doorway and looked out. My two horses glanced curiously at me over the corral fence. My partially filled wagon stood in its place beside the mill. No one else was anywhere in sight.

I scratched my head. I must be more homesick than I thought. The words could only have come from my mind with such longing that I thought it was the voice of someone else speaking to me.

I looked critically at the wood stacked in the wagon, calculating how much I already had and how much more I would need. Maybe there was enough. Maybe I should go home now. I surely wanted to. I was tired clear to my bones.

I sighed deeply. I really should finish the job and save myself another trip. I was already here, sweaty and tired, but ready to do what needed to be done.

I walked across the floor and again bent to my task. "Go home." This time I didn't even look up. I'd never heard my thoughts this clearly before, as though someone else was speaking to me. It was unusual, but I was too busy to wonder about it. Every pause stole my momentum, requiring more energy to get back to work. The familiar buzz of the saw and earthy smell of sawdust sifting to the floor at my feet triggered a wave of gratitude that I was able to work and take care of my family.

"Go home." This time, the insistent voice shot through me, sucking the strength from my limbs. My arms and legs began to tremble as though the bones had gone soft. I straightened. Abandoning my project, I turned and followed my feet out the door. I was going home.

I unhooked a bridle from a nail on the side of the mill and slid it over the bay horse's head, the one I called "Skitter." I worked quickly, some premonition within me warning that I shouldn't even take time to hitch up both horses to the wagon. I no longer questioned the feeling I had, but swung up onto

Skitter's back and clenched my knees around her belly. I nudged her sides and she trotted through the open gate, heading out across the valley at an easy pace. The other horse was free to follow or find her own circuitous route back to the fort. I had only one goal in mind, and I didn't look back.

Before we had even gone a mile, my leg muscles tightened into Skitter's sides, urging her faster. For some unknown purpose, from an uncertain source, I was being urged to greater speed. I kicked Skitter into a gallop and leaned over her neck, straining toward home.

I matched my body to the horse's gait, realizing that strength had returned to my legs, keeping me astride the galloping horse. Skitter headed straight across the valley, barely bothering to dodge the sagebrush that stood between her and home.

Skitter's sides were heaving and there was the damp of sweat between her back and the seat of my trousers when the fort at last came into view. The long rays of the sun were slanting across from the west as I rode up to the fort. When I slid to the ground, Mary came running out from between the heavy wooden doors of the gate.

"John!" she called in a choked voice. She ran headlong toward me, tear tracks shining on her cheeks. I gathered her into my arms. She didn't even pull back from my sweaty shirt. My heart dropped in sudden fear. Something must be wrong with the children.

I held my wife tightly against me. "Mary," I said, my heart in my throat. "What's wrong?"

"Indians," she choked out past her tears.

My heart leapt to attention. "Here?" I asked. I pushed her away and searched her face. "Hazard? Sarah?"

Mary shook her head and dashed her hand at her eyes. "The children are fine," she assured me. She flashed a wobbly smile before she said, "It was you I was worried about."

"Me?" I was astonished.

"Look!" Mary said, pulling on my sleeve as she pointed behind me. I turned to look.

My heart lurched at the unexpected glow in the canyon mouth, an undulating wave of color that pulsed a scared heart-beat of red and orange and yellow. My legs again grew weak as I realized it was coming from the exact spot where the sawmill stood.

Mary clung to my arm. "When the Indian warning reached the fort, I had a terrible feeling about you. I prayed and prayed that you would come home." In spite of the warmth from the setting sun, a chill ran up both my arms and settled at the nape of my neck, standing my hair on end.

To the Indians, the sawmill was a white man's scar upon their land. I trembled. A voice had told me three times to go home. What if I hadn't finally obeyed? All the wood that was now turning to ash alongside the mill was nothing compared to my life. How narrowly had I missed being caught in the sawmill's funeral pyre?

"Let's go in, John," Mary said, tugging at my hand. I gripped Skitter's reins and we hurried into the safety of the fort, which was hardly any protection at all when compared to the safety of prayer.

*Kathy B. Ockey reports the story of John Henry, his wife, Mary, and children Hazard and Sarah from a sketch of the life of John Henry Owen Wilcox. In the summer of about 1853, John traveled with a party of men to the sawmill across the valley to cut lumber. The cooperative venture finished, the other men left John behind to complete his personal project of getting lumber for his garden fence.*

*Meanwhile, John's wife Mary received word that the Indians were on the warpath. Worried, Mary prayed for her husband's safety.*

*John was hard at work when he heard a voice say, "Go home." Surprised, he looked around but saw no one. The second time, he ignored the voice. The third time it was so insistent that John quit working and immediately left for home. A feeling overtook him that urged him to ride faster. Before John reached the fort, an orange glow from the burning mill behind him highlighted the sky. His tearful wife welcomed him to safety* (Saga of the Sanpitch, *Vol. 10, pg. 23).*

# KEEPING COOL

The day started out strange from the minute mama woke me up and dressed me in my Sunday dress. Even though I was only four years old, I was pretty sure it wasn't Sunday, but when Mama and Papa put on their Sunday clothes, I thought maybe I was mistaken.

We all got into the buggy and started down the road. Warm early morning air brushed my cheeks, promising to turn hot as the day wore on. I didn't want to sit through a stuffy church meeting, so I was mighty pleased and surprised when Papa turned the horses toward Grandma's instead of toward the meetinghouse. "Where are we going?" I asked.

"To Uncle Hallie's viewing," Mama said.

"Who's Uncle Hallie?" I asked. "What's a viewing?"

"Uncle Hallie is Grandma's older brother," Mama said. "His spirit went to live in heaven, but his body's still here."

I opened my eyes wide. Was Mama teasing me? How could someone be in two places at the same time? Mama smiled at my expression. "Lots of people who loved Uncle Hallie are going to come see him at Grandma's to say goodbye."

"Lots of people?" I asked. I looked down the road and saw Grandma's house grow steadily closer as the patient horse clip-clopped down the road. I could only see one buggy parked in front, and it looked like Uncle Alfred and Aunt Ginny's. They weren't lots of people. Counting my bigger cousin, Robert, they were only three.

"The people will come later," Mama explained. "We're early to help Grandma get the food ready."

"What's the food for?" I asked.

"Everyone will be hungry after the funeral," Mama said.

I didn't know what a funeral was, but I didn't bother to ask, because Papa pulled to a stop in front of Grandma's house. I scrambled down from the seat and ran toward the front door.

94

"Eunice! Walk!" Mama reprimanded me. I was surprised. Did I have to act like it was church just because I had my Sunday dress on? It didn't seem fair, but I slowed down just before I let myself inside Grandma's house.

I stopped as dead as a doornail and stared at a long black box, set inside a huge metal tub, resting on two sawhorses smack dab in the middle of Grandma's living room. The box was at least as big as a watering trough, but it had a lid on it. I couldn't figure out what it was for, because no horses could drink from a closed trough, and Grandma would never let any horses into her living room anyway.

"Help!" a muffled voice sounded from inside the box. My heart started thumping real uncomfortable inside my chest. Someone must be trapped inside that watering trough! I wondered with mounting horror if it might be full of water, too. I would have opened the lid, but it was too high for me to reach.

"Help! Let me out!" the same voice called.

"Papa!" I yelled, clasping my hands together in helpless horror. "Help!"

It wasn't Papa who answered my cry, but Grandma. She came out of the kitchen, wiping her hands on a towel. "Whatever are you hollering about, child?"

I pointed my finger up at the black box. "Someone's in there!" I said.

Grandma shook her head sadly. "I know, dear. It's Uncle Hallie."

"You have to let him out!" I yelled.

Grandma drew back and her eyes widened. "Why, Eunice, what has gotten into you?"

Just then the voice snickered softly. "Listen!" I said, pulling my hands apart and grabbing onto Grandma's apron. "Uncle Hallie is laughing!"

Papa and Mama pushed through the door, baskets and hampers in their arms.

Grandma confronted them with her hands on her hips. "What have you been telling this child?" she asked brusquely.

Mama looked confused. "Just that we were coming to Uncle Hallie's viewing," she said.

"Excuse me, ladies, I've got to set this down in the kitchen," Papa said as he hefted the big hamper in his arms. "I'll be back in a minute." He started toward the kitchen door.

Grandma didn't wait for him. "Why is it that Eunice thinks we have to let Uncle Hallie out of his coffin?" Grandma asked.

Mama cast a sharp look at me. I was just getting ready to explain that Uncle Hallie had called for help, when Papa said, "Well, Robert, what are you doing down there? Be a good lad and jump up and get the door for me. That's a good boy."

Robert stood up from behind the trough and opened the kitchen door for Papa.

"Robert!" I called, grateful to have a witness. "You heard Uncle Hallie, didn't you? He said he needed help, and he wanted to get out! Go on, tell them!"

To my disgust, Robert didn't answer. He just looked down at his shoes.

"Robert," Grandma said. "Were you playing a joke on Eunice? How could you? I'll teach you to have some respect for the dead!"

Grandma strode over to Robert and grabbed his ear. I winced in sympathy. Grandma turned back to me. "Eunice, Uncle Hallie wasn't speaking from his coffin. It was Robert, pretending he was Uncle Hallie. Now, don't you worry about a thing. Uncle Hallie is resting peacefully."

Grandma pulled Robert through the kitchen door. "Now you just come and tell your mother what you did!" she scolded.

Mama followed Grandma into the kitchen. I thought I might follow and see what Robert was in for, but just then the front door opened again and Uncle Albert came through it with a bucket in each hand. The buckets were full of lumpy white rocks. "Hi, Eunice!" Uncle Albert called cheerfully, and then he walked across the room and dumped the rocks into the huge metal tub.

"What are you doing?" I asked.

"I'm keeping Uncle Hallie cool," Uncle Albert said. He set

down the buckets and lifted the lid of the trough. "I've got to go get more," he said, picking the buckets up off the floor and heading outside again.

I stood on my toes to see inside the trough, but I was still too short. Robert came back into the living room, rubbing his ear. His eyes brightened when he saw me. "Hey, do you want to see?" he asked.

"Yes!" I answered.

Robert stood behind me and wrapped his arms around my waist, but before he could boost me up, the front door opened again. "Stop it, Robert!" a big girl said, hurrying over and taking hold of my arm. "She's too little!"

"She wanted to see," Robert answered sullenly, relaxing his grip. I was terribly disappointed.

The big girl talked to me in baby talk that was awfully hard to understand. I didn't like her, not even after she told me she was my cousin, Maude, who had traveled clear from the city to be here for Uncle Hallie's viewing.

Before long, more and more people came. Every time someone opened Grandma's door, hot air from outside would leak in, making Grandma's house as stuffy as church.

Some of the kids who came were little like me and some were bigger like Robert and Maude. Maude said they were all my cousins. I didn't know if I should believe her, because I'd never seen some of them before in my whole entire life.

There were lots of solemn adults who sat or stood around the room in dark-clothed groups. Ladies were waving pieces of paper back and forth in front of their faces. Some of the men used their hats to fan the hot summer air, dabbing their brows with handkerchiefs as they murmured among themselves. One lady had a store-bought fan tucked up inside a wooden handle. When she spread it out, a soft green weeping willow tree unfolded, and brightly colored birds took flight across the accordion folds. I'd never seen anything so pretty. I stared at her fanning herself for a long time.

When I finally turned away, I pushed my hair up off my

damp forehead. Then I noticed Robert sucking on a small white rock, like the kind Uncle Albert had dumped beside the trough. I'd tasted rocks before, and I hadn't found them worth eating. One of the other cousins looked at Robert and asked, "Watcha got?"

Robert answered him without taking the rock out of his mouth, which made his voice come out kind of hollow and awkward. "Ice."

The other boy's eyes went wide with envy. "Where'd you get it?"

Robert stuck his hand down beside the casket and came up with another chunk of white ice. He handed it over. All the other cousins soon crowded around, helping themselves to lumps of refreshing ice and sliding them into their mouths, giggling as they sucked the cold out.

Someone put a piece in my hand. The unexpected cold shot through my fingers and I dropped the ice like a hot rock. I looked up at all the bigger kids wearing contented smiles as they quietly slurped their ice chunks. I looked at my ice on the floor, then bent over and scooped it up. Copying the others, I put the end of the ice into my mouth. It was too big for me to fit it in all at once, so I held it like a piece broken off an all-day sucker.

At first it was so cold it almost hurt, but when the ice melted into wonderfully cool water and ran down my throat, I could see why the other kids were smiling. I soon discovered that if I moved the ice from hand to hand, it kept my fingers from getting too cold.

Melted ice water was running down my arms when a lady shrieked so loudly she made me jump and drop my ice again. "What are you doing?" the lady screamed. Some of the children quickly tossed their ice chunks back in beside the coffin, but mine was on the floor, so I couldn't do that.

"The children, the children!" the loud lady yelled. Several grownups stood up and came closer to see what all the ruckus was about. Grandma pushed past them and stood over us, a deep frown lining her face. When she planted her hands on her hips,

I knew we were in big trouble. Quickly, I covered the back of my skirt with my hands, hoping to ward off a spanking.

"You children march yourselves out of here, right now!" she barked. "Get outside and don't set foot back inside this house until I say so!" My chin quivered. I didn't like to be yelled at any more than I liked to be spanked.

Maude took hold of my hand and we hurried past the unsmiling grownups to the hot outside air. What were they so mad about? We hadn't eaten all of the ice. There was plenty left if they wanted some.

We huddled together in the shade of a tree, but it still felt hotter than blazes. I sure wished I'd kept hold of my ice. Dry gusts of wind blew dirt into my eyes. I rubbed them and let the tears come. I was miserable.

It seemed a long time before the grownups came outside. When they did, several of the men carried the long black box out with them. After they slid it onto a wagon, my Papa found me and carried me to the cemetery where the box named Uncle Hallie was lowered into the ground. The men shoveled too much dirt onto it. By the time they finally stopped, there was a big hump of earth over the top of Uncle Hallie. By now I was so hot and hungry that I was sorry I'd ever gone anywhere near that old coffin.

Back at Grandma's house, she made us kids stay outside until after all the adults had gotten their food. I was glad when Robert worked the water pump so we could take turns getting a drink. Some of the boys stuck their heads under the faucet, wetting their hair until it came out dripping. They shook their heads like wet dogs and splashed water on everyone. That made me laugh.

Finally, Grandma called us kids to come inside and get some food, then she made us take our plates outside to eat on the porch. We tried to keep flies away with one hand while we ate with the other.

By the time Papa came to get me, I'd decided that the next time Mama brought out my best clothes, I'd make sure it was

Sunday. And the next time I saw a long black box like Uncle Hallie's, I'd run into the next room and wouldn't come out until somebody took it away and buried it.

*Margaret Riding tells a story her mother, Virginia Nielson, told her about a coffin that came in on a train. The people on the platform were startled to hear a voice coming from inside the coffin, saying, "Let me out! Let me out!" They soon traced the cry for help to a teenage culprit, a boy who was throwing his voice just for the enjoyment of putting a scare into everyone!*

*Eunice McCurdy recalls a viewing at Grandpa Hans Christian Hansen and Grandma Annie Margaret's house on a summer day in the early 1900's when she was four years old. The children soon discovered that Uncle Hallie's casket was packed with ice and shared it amongst themselves. Eunice was unable to reach the ice for herself, but some well-meaning cousin gave her a piece, so along with the older cousins, she was considered guilty, too, and worthy of punishment (Saga of the Sanpitch, Vol. 21 pg. 37).*

# VOICES

Grimly, I faced the deserted lane, the road to absolutely nowhere. The sun slowly pulled its light down with it behind the west mountains. I didn't relish walking this road home at any time of day, but especially not in the darkening evening.

This was all Pa's fault. He wouldn't even seriously consider my suggestion to move to town. He was such an old fossil! With great maturity and perfect reasoning, I had explained to him that our family could live in a house in town and he could still work the land. It wouldn't be any trouble for him to ride his horse out to the farm every day.

"But, Shirley, my girl, I like to keep my eye on things," he'd said. Then he'd winked at me. He was positively infuriating! He had no idea what it was like to be fifteen years old and live miles and miles away from town.

It wasn't enough that I was burdened down with my books for the half-mile walk. I'd stayed late for the first school play rehearsal, and when that was over, my teacher had given me a quilt to return to Mama. We had forgotten it at the Labor Day picnic, so it had been stored it in the school closet until Mrs. Allred remembered to give it back.

With my arms full and my house nowhere in sight, I figured I might as well have been walking across the plains with the pioneers. I sighed and my soul filled with an over-flowing measure of self-pity. I wasn't as fortunate as a pioneer. I was treated like one of the oxen, a mere beast of burden.

Dwelling on the injustice of it all soon chased away the pity. Thrusting my jaw forward, I made a firm resolve right then and there that when I grew up, I would live in town. No house out in the fields for me. I would put myself squarely in the middle of everything, where I could easily walk to the theater, the store, the community dances, or my friend's houses. I would be a regular social butterfly once I broke free of the cocoon that bound me to the family farm.

Feeling better for the rock-solid promise I'd made to myself, I cradled my books in one arm, threw the old quilt over my shoulder with the other, and started resolutely down the dirt road toward home.

"Ooooooh." A low moan stopped me as suddenly as if I'd run into a wall, sending an unwelcome shiver sliding down my back as quick as a startled mouse. I threw an uneasy glance over my shoulder, slowly turning in a circle. I scanned the fields, but I couldn't see anyone. Was someone hiding in the weeds by the road, trying to scare me?

After a breathless moment of silence, I overcame my temporary paralysis and dared to move down the road again, my eyes darting from side to side. The pitiful moan floated over the air again, brushing the back of my neck with cold chills and halting me in my tracks. I whipped my head around, desperate to find the source of the sound. The road was still empty.

Maybe this wasn't a prank. Maybe someone was really hurt, concealed in the growth by the side of the road. I swallowed hard, my heart fluttering in panic. If they were hurt so badly that they couldn't even stand, there might be blood. The thought made me queasy, but my imagination didn't stop. There could be broken bones, maybe even the kind that stuck out through ragged and bleeding skin.

"Oooooaaaie!" This time the moan ended in a shrieking high note of hysteria. I let out a little shriek in return, then clamped my hand over my mouth. I had to get help. In spite of everything I carried, I began to trot down the road toward home. If someone was hurt as badly as it sounded, I needed to get my parents quickly.

My thoughts were broken by a groan, heavy with sorrow that weighed down my soul. My legs slowed and my head tilted in confusion. This voice was distinctly different from the moan. Knees trembling, my frightened mind tried to make sense of it. Were there two injured people? The groan sounded again, loud and insistent, from somewhere above my head. Dread shot through me and I ducked my head. Shoulders hunched, I risked a look up toward the horrifying sound.

There was no one hovering in the air above me—at least no one I could see. All that met my fearful gaze was a malicious half moon hanging low in the sky, glaring down at me with an angry squint.

Propelled now by raw fear, I hurried down the road. Terror crawled up my back with icy fingers, prickling the hairs on my neck with sharp claws of fear. The ominous groaning measured my every step. The moan that had arrested me at the head of the lane cut pitifully through the evening air in duet with the groans.

A sudden realization shot a chill of new fright to the very marrow of my bones. How was it possible for the moaning voice to belong to a severely injured person if it was shadowing me? My mouth went dry, and I hugged the books to my chest so tightly they all but bruised my flesh. My legs were shaking so badly, I couldn't see how they held me up, except that I was too terrified to collapse. The invisible cries continued tormenting me as I hurried along the dusky road toward home.

My waking nightmare intensified when more anguished voices joined in as though I'd suddenly found myself walking next to a medieval dungeon full of terrified prisoners in agony, hopeless for any relief from their misery except death. A sudden shriek of despair sounded so close to my ear that it shredded my nerves and nearly sent me out of my skin. My knees quaked so badly that I was afraid I'd fall down and never get up again. I could feel the expression of horror molded onto my face as stiff and unyielding as cold candle wax.

I didn't know what was happening, but I wanted it to stop. I quickly tugged the quilt over my head with a trembling hand. I gathered the fabric close around my face, willing the familiar old quilt to somehow soothe the terrible fright that coursed through me in ever increasing waves of alarm. I only allowed one eye enough freedom to keep me to the center of the road and away from the dark undergrowth along the roadside. The less I saw and heard, the better I liked it.

The quilt muffled the groans and tortured shrieks that haunted my every step, but I could still hear them. Whatever was haunting me was still there. Without stopping, I closed my eyes against the unearthly cries that came at me from every direction. Now my mind was free to imagine the horribly desperate voices accompanied by claw-like hands reaching for me, grabbing at my skirt. Once the grip was secure, the unseen hands could drag me back to wherever they were coming from.

I yanked the quilt off and my eyes flew open, checking the road in all directions. Empty. The darkness was deepening, and the deafening voices continued their wordless laments.

I wondered desperately why my home wasn't in sight. Surely I should have reached it by now. I threw frightened glances over both shoulders. I could still see no one and nothing in the gloom that crowded up behind me.

Gradually, a new sound blended with the moans and tortured cries. My poor body quaked with dread. What was next? I didn't think I could take any more! I squinted into the dusk, listening hard past my frantic, ragged breathing. The new noise was the creek. The swift, cold current cut across the road under the old wooden bridge that marked the halfway point home, adding its sinister chuckle to the haunting voices. The frigid water sparkled with hard bits of white moonlight. The moaning, groaning voices crowded desperately around me, punctuated by shrieks that chilled my blood.

Should I turn back? Would I be safer heading toward town than continuing home on this lonely, haunted road? In town I might find someone to bring me back on a horse swift enough to outrun these unseen tormented ones. Yet if I turned back, what was I to gain? What might I find back along the road now?

Suddenly, a warm light bloomed beside the road up ahead. I stared at it, relief washing through me and breaking the knot of fear in my chest. The light was coming from the kitchen window of my house, where Mother would be cooking supper within safe and familiar walls. All thoughts of turning back to escape the voices fled. I was going home.

I stepped onto the bridge, nearly deafened by the protests of the faceless things that followed me. The banks that imprisoned the rushing water yawned open like a mouth hungry for warm and living flesh to tumble over its rock-strewn tongue. After the life and breath was sucked out of its victim, it would spit it out, as cold as a dead fish.

I had to grip the handrail as my quivering legs carried me across the old bridge. The shrieking voices protested every step, and each breath I took was a prayer that my knees wouldn't give out and pitch me into the icy water. I stumbled onto the far bank, my eyes riveted on the warm lights of home.

The moans and shrieks were quieter from this side of the bridge, growing more subdued and hopeless in their distraught cries for either relief or vengeance. The wails trailed thinly after me as I made a dash for my house.

My hand on the kitchen doorknob at last, I threw one more look around at nothing but empty night punctuated by a glaring slice of moon. I quickly twisted the knob and slipped inside to warmth, light, and safety. I firmly shut the darkness and the voices out.

Although I had to walk that road home for several more years, I never heard the voices again, and I never found out where they came from or why they were calling to me.

*In the early 1900s, Shirley Reynolds Burnside faced a half-mile walk along Beck's Lane in Chester, Utah, every day after school. One autumn evening, as a girl of fifteen, she was fright-ened when she heard moaning, groaning and wailing as she began her walk home. The disembodied voices seemed to come from the very air around her. Throwing a blanket over her head only added to her anxiety.*

*At a bridge that marked the halfway point, the voices got so loud that the teenager thought of turning back. Yet the safety of home was in sight. After she hurried over the water, the voices faded, but still followed her to her door. Once inside, the voices stilled. Shirley never figured out the source of the sounds, and she never heard them again* (Saga of the Sanpitch, *Vol. 30,* pg. 36).

# THE CLARION HAUNT

My thigh muscle screamed for relief, but I couldn't let up on the brake. The horses stepped stiff-legged down the steep mountain road, checking the descent of the heavy lumber-laden wagon while trying to avoid being run over themselves.

I grimaced with the effort of standing on the foot brake to keep it from slipping. I clung to the reins with hands sore from broken blisters. This homesteading life was a different kind of hardship from what I'd known before. It certainly was no harder than surviving the Russian Revolution.

The opportunity to homestead had sounded like heaven after the hell I'd lived through in a country that wasn't kind to Jews like me even in the best of times. When I finally left the day-to-day fight to survive behind me and boarded a boat to America, I thought I was leaving all my struggles behind. When I reached Philadelphia, instead of streets paved with gold, I found streets full of filth and slums with big rats that fed on garbage and dead animals that perished in the dark alleys from fighting or starvation.

Although better that animals killed each other than people, there were still murders, robbings and beatings among men. The slums weren't the land of plenty and opportunity that I'd expected.

Then I read an offer in the paper for forty acres of good farmland to each of those willing to travel across the country to Utah and work the land. My imagination was seized with images of green fields and flowing streams, neatly painted wooden houses and picket fences.

I was tireless in recruiting a sizeable number of Jewish families to take advantage of this golden opportunity along with me. We would have our own community in the wide open spaces, finally living in peace after generations of persecution that had followed our people. It seemed that God was granting us blessings after all. Now all we had to do was get across the country, plant our crops, reap the harvest, and live out our lives in green and growing plenty.

The Mormons had proved that Zion could be established in the Utah wilderness. In their struggle to escape their own persecution, they had developed empathy for what our Jewish culture had endured for centuries, and would now welcome us.

Ah, Zion! It had turned out to be more work than I had anticipated, but who gets anything for free? I was an enthusiastic volunteer for my own acreage, looking forward to living on this wild land instead of among the wild gangs of men that roamed the dark streets of the big city.

Now we were here, in our own little town of Clarion. I was on my way home from the mountains with a load of wood to share with my neighbors who were desperately trying to scratch a living out of the hard desert soil.

Bumping down the mountain road, I remembered my first glimpse of the city called Gunnison, the houses clustered together in the hub of a wheel with the farmland thrown out around it like spokes of green and gold. We people of Clarion had settled west of Gunnison, with individual plots of forty acres, our houses built right on our own land. As a result of this bold new plan, we were strung out along eight miles at the base of the West Mountains. Although the idea was that living and farming your own plot would help you to develop a feel for the land and an ability to grow better crops, it was hard to bond together when you had to ride a horse to your neighbor's to borrow a cup of sugar.

Yet this plan could work. It had to work. It was the best chance we'd been given in our entire lives.

There were some who had begun talking in synagogue of giving up and leaving. A couple of families had lost their faith in our settlement and had already packed their few belongings into wagons and driven to the train station. Yet how could God bless us if we didn't give our all, trust in Him and turn our lives over to His hands?

It was true that the water system wasn't working as we had hoped it would. The first time we'd filled the cistern with water, one of the walls had collapsed. All the wells we dug were dry. Yet God had tested Abraham's faith to the last moment and spared Isaac. We could yet be spared.

I pulled back on the reins as my horses tossed their heads. They didn't like me riding the wagon right on their tails, and neither did I. I didn't know how else to get down the steep mountain slope, so I kept my foot on the brake and gripped the reins more tightly.

Getting wood at least gave me something to show for my labors. I wasn't any more successful at farming than the others, but I refused to give up. I made myself do the chores I wasn't good at and didn't like to do, because they had to be done. In order for Clarion to survive, everyone had to persevere. No one could give up or we would all suffer.

Things would improve if only it would rain. I risked a glance up at the hot, cloudless blue sky, thinking how ironic it was that a city like Philadelphia received bounteous rain, while in this place of earth and seeds, nature was stingy with the necessary water to make things grow. I gritted my teeth in frustration. There had to be a way to make our settlement prosper.

One horse stumbled, pulling my mind back to my task. Suddenly the wagon surged ahead. I yelled at the same time the horses squealed in fear, panicked hooves scrabbling as they veered awkwardly to the side in a vain effort to escape the top-heavy wagon. It lurched sideways and slowly tipped over.

I could feel myself falling, but was helpless to stop. As if my life had slowed before my eyes, I saw the first few logs roll off and skitter down the mountain road. Then I tipped off balance, my arms spread in a desperate attempt to break my fall. In the end, it didn't matter how I landed. The load of wood rolled steadily out of the overturned wagon, burying me alive.

The intense pain of snapping bones and bruising flesh forced a scream out of my lungs, but mercifully, the pain was short lived. I managed to stand up and survey the wreckage of timbers.

The road was completely blocked. I would need help with this.

Just as I turned away to go recruit some muscle, something out of the ordinary caught my eye. I stepped closer, squinting at the object, then my eyes flew wide in disbelief. It couldn't be. But it was. I couldn't deny that the boot sticking out from under the tangled logs was my own. When I looked closer, I saw that my foot was still in it. I just about fell over when I realized that my broken, lifeless body was buried under that wreckage of timbers. I was dead.

I went to my funeral. Everyone said real nice things about me. I was buried on a hill overlooking the town of Gunnison, with a tall gravestone carved in both Hebrew and English. It was more than I'd ever expected. I was truly touched.

Even though I was dead, I didn't look to move on to the next world. I was unwilling to leave this place that I had so fiercely determined to make my home, and that I had died for. I was delighted to discover that my movements were unrestricted, but I was frustrated that my entreaties to my fellow Jews to stay and work the land were totally ignored. It was as if I was invisible to them, even though I could see them plain as day. Since they couldn't hear me giving them encouragement and good advice, they all eventually left our Zion, abandoning our ideal brotherhood community of Clarion.

With heavy heart, I watched the property that had once been in the names of my friends auctioned off, even down to the houses, which were moved from their foundations and hauled to other locations in the valley. The land fell into the hands of Gentiles, who were unaware that there was one Jew who refused to give up and leave.

It was a wonder to me when I saw the Gentiles begin to drive their farm machinery all by itself while the horses stood in the pastures and watched. I marveled at the watering systems that were installed, pipes and sprinklers working like a miracle to spray out the life-giving water that we had been so sorely lacking. This wondrous creation made it so that a few farmers could work vast amounts of land. I inspected them frequently, amazed at the inventions that would have saved my fellow countrymen their dream of a prosperous community, if only we'd had them earlier.

I gradually became used to being invisible to everyone except animals, and comfortable with coming and going as I pleased, so it was a great shock to me when I was moving across a farm yard one afternoon and a Gentile on a horseless farm machine stopped and stared at me. His eyes clearly followed my progress as I moved behind a windbreak. I stood among the trees and watched him, feeling somehow vulnerable now that someone could see me. The cows looked curious, no doubt wondering when I was going to move along. The Gentile sat still for a few moments before he again rolled his machine down the road, casting frequent nervous glances my way.

I followed his progress to a house that had been recently built nearly in the center of the old business district of Clarion, the businesses being a synagogue, store, and schoolhouse. What extravagance that seemed now, with only this single family and a herd of cows left to walk across the empty foundations of what had been Clarion town.

Now that I'd been seen, I felt a great curiosity about this family. I harbored a kinship in my heart with them and realized that I liked the old sense of belonging that I'd been missing for so long. Feeling as though I was all but a member of the family, I overcame my reticence and took opportunities to walk through their house. The doors were wonderfully lightweight with smooth, round knobs that turned easily and latched securely with an effortless push of the door.

I found several amazing machines outside their house, the kind that moved without a horse. I explored them thoroughly, giving myself a delightful fright when I managed to make them roar to life. The woman of the house came to the door and looked over at me, but I could see that she was looking right through me. I turned the machine off and she ducked back into the house, her eyes wide with fear.

On a different day, another woman was in the yard. She

stopped suddenly and looked around, her frightened gaze going right through me. I don't know how she knew I was there since she obviously couldn't see me, but her two dogs gave me a furtive glance before they ran and hid, even though I meant them no harm.

One night I noticed a visitor walking across the yard. He was almost to the picket fence when I decided to give him a hand and save him the bother of opening the gate. I lifted him over the fence and set him down on the other side, but his legs wouldn't hold him up. He landed on his back, staring up with an expression of such surprise that I laughed about it for days.

A few years later, the family sold their farm and moved to Gunnison. At first I was disappointed and lonely, but now the house is all mine. I can open and close the doors to my heart's content, and when I get bored with that, I look out the window and imagine that I can see the town of Clarion set on the new green fields, the sprinklers spraying their blasts of life-giving water in large arcs over the ghostly homes in my mind.

*Morris Reid tells of a time in the winter of 1978 when he was driving south on the old dirt farm road that led to the former business district of Clarion, where he built his house. He saw a tall, white object moving through the feedlot off to his left. At first he thought it was snow caught up in a whirlwind, but quickly realized there was no wind. Looking more closely, he noticed a round head shape at the top of a rectangle that vaguely resembled a body. The object moved behind a wind-break and didn't come out again.*

*A year later, his daughter Teresa was looking out the bay window of their house and saw the same thing moving across the field from the Jewish side of old Clarion town and traveling northward.*

*His wife Bonnie confirmed that there were times when she was alone in the house and the bathroom and bedroom doors would open and shut of their own accord.*

*One day, Bonnie heard a motor. Thinking her son had come*

*home, she stepped outside before she realized that the running motor belonged to a boat parked beside the house. No one was there besides Bonnie. On another occasion when Bonnie went outside to check on a running motor, she discovered the empty car idling without a key in the ignition. As she backed into the house, the car motor died.*

*Bonnie's sister-in-law was riding in a jeep on the back roads and saw a tall white shape move over a hill and disappear.*

*Bonnie's mother was outside exercising with the two family dogs when she was seized with a sudden chill that made her shiver. A cold premonition that someone was watching washed over her at the same moment one dog dove under a trailer and the other dog bolted inside the house.*

*A man who refused to be named claims he was walking across a Clarion yard at night when he was lifted up over a picket fence and dropped onto the ground on the other side by a tall, ghostly pillar of white.*

*A Jewish man named Aaron Binder came to Utah from Philadelphia after immigrating from post-revolution Russia to help settle Clarion in 1912. He was killed while transporting a load of lumber that tippoed over on the mountainside. His headstone is next to that of a baby boy, who died of unknown causes. The Jewish section of Clarion was basically abandoned by the year 1914, leaving behind Aaron Binder and the ten-month-old Edward Lieberman buried on a barren and lonely hill that overlooks the city of Gunnison.*

# ONE GOOD TURN

I had to be the last person on earth. It was the only explanation that made sense. I hadn't seen another living being for days and days, and now it seemed forever since the snow had begun falling, working relentlessly to bury me alive. My hopeless heart could think of no other explanation except that there wasn't any one else beyond the frozen whiteness piling up against my log cabin tomb. I stared out the window, my eyes unfocused and my mind turned inward, stumbling around the desperate ache of slow starvation. What am I doing here?

The question came unbidden, without anger or recrimination. Even as I asked, I knew the answer. Love had brought me here. I loved Rick more than a gingerbread-trimmed house in town with warm fires blazing in every hearth, more than a pantry stocked with readily available food from the general store, more than a pianoforte, indeed, more than anything on earth. That's why I was sitting alone on this homestead in the wild and beautiful Teton Mountains.

While my parents approved of Rick, they didn't approve of his lifestyle. They had feared for both my safety and my sanity when he had told them of his dream to homestead lush meadow acreage in a remote Teton valley. They had done their best to persuade him to take a job in town instead. To Rick's credit, he had listened to them before discussing the matter with me. As he spoke to me of living and working in town, the light in his eyes faded and his countenance drooped. I looked across the table into his weary face, giving in to a sudden surge of compassion. He was willing to work a job he didn't like and live where he didn't want to just for me. What he didn't know is that I wouldn't be happy unless he was.

"Rick," I'd said, taking one of his hands in both of mine.

"Yes, Asa," he said, looking at me with strange, dull eyes that didn't belong on my beloved's face.

"I know what I want to do."

I could see him stiffen as he braced himself for my words. "What?"

A slow smile crept over my face. "I think we should homestead."

Rick's mouth dropped open and his eyes lit up. "Really, Asa? You really want to?"

If I'd had any doubts before, seeing his face come alive quenched them all. "Yes," I said, unable to stop from smiling. "I want to homestead with you."

So here I was, two days ride from town, homemaking in a rough log cabin that Rick and I had built ourselves on a spread that was as beautiful as heaven must be. In the summer, a stream of pure water tumbled through the meadow close to the cabin, and trees stood as sentries along the mountain wall that protected our little valley from winds that would otherwise cripple cornstalks and batter wheat grass down flat.

In the six months we'd been married, I hadn't felt deprived of neighbors. Rick was all I needed. We had the occasional Indians stopping by, curious folk who had never been threatening. Even so, the first sight of them always gave me a start. Rick was never afraid.

Usually I went with Rick on his trips to town. I liked to see what was new in the general store and catch up on the news, but the last time he'd gone, I was the way of women, and suffering from cramps. The last thing I wanted to do was ride a horse.

Rick had been three days late getting home. I paced the floor, imagining his broken body lying at the bottom of some ravine. I checked out the window hundreds of times a day, wondering with a catch in my heart if he'd been waylaid and beaten by robbers who stole his horse and clothes before leaving him wounded and defenseless in the wilderness.

At last, when my fingernails were chewed down to the quick, I saw him riding up the trail through a halo of sun-brightened autumn leaves. I burst from the house and ran to meet him. He swung off his horse and threw his muscular arms around my waist, hugging me so hard that my feet left the ground. I had a pretty good stranglehold around his neck, too.

When we finally broke apart, he began untying bundles from the back of his patient pack horse, shooting me frequent looks that melted my heart down into my toes. "I was scared to death," I said as I opened my arms for a bag of rice. "Why were you gone so long?"

"On my way to town I came across an old Indian lying on the mountainside," he said. He slung a full saddlebag over one of his shoulders and hefted a sack of sugar in the other. "The man was so sick and weak, he could barely move."

I hurried ahead of Rick and opened the cabin door. As soon as we'd dropped our supplies onto the table, I asked, "What was the matter?"

Rick shook his head. "I don't know. He looked awfully old. His face was all wrinkles, and the lines from his nose to his mouth were deep as canyons." Rick linked my hand in his and we walked outside. "Funny thing is, he had a bow and quiver of arrows with him, like he was out hunting, although it didn't seem he'd be able to get around well even on a good day."

Rick took up the horse's reins and we headed toward the barn. "What happened to him?" I asked.

"I put him on my horse and walked until I found his village," Rick said. "The tribe came running when they saw us. Seems they'd missed him and were getting ready to go out looking when we showed up. Once they took over and he was settled, they insisted I stay and eat with them." Rick squeezed my hand as we entered the barn. "They can't cook anywhere near as good as you can, Asa, but I didn't want to hurt their feelings, so I stayed."

Rick let go of my hand so he could loosen the saddle. "I wouldn't have expected anything less of you," I said, my heart warming at the goodness of this man I was lucky enough to call my husband.

When our provisions again ran low and Rick was ready to

make another supply run, I told him I didn't want to go. He turned startled eyes to me. "Why not?"

"I just don't feel like it," I hedged.

He'd shot me a look full of such hurt that I blurted, "How am I supposed to surprise you if you're always hanging around?"

"Surprise?" he asked. Really, his open mouthed expression was quite comical.

"Look here," I said as patiently as I could. "It's nearly Christmas. If you don't know what that means, then I'm not going to explain it to you. You'll just have to wait and see. Now get out of here and stop asking questions!"

Rick's face cleared and he flashed me an adorable smile. "Well, if that's the way you feel about it, I'll just get out of here," he said.

"You do that," I said.

He stepped close to me and said, "I should be back in four or five days."

"I know that," I said.

Rick moved his face closer to mine. "The sooner gone, the sooner I get back," he said softly. Then he kissed me, warm and long. I sighed with happiness as he broke away and swung up onto his horse. He tipped his hat to me before he turned and rode down the trail.

When I went to the cupboard to make supper, I was dismayed to find that the mice had gotten into the flour and rice, and had somehow managed to tip over the molasses jar. Sweet brown goo stained the rough wooden boards in my cupboard. I recoiled at the sight that bore a disturbingly close resemblance to spilled blood. I managed to salvage a cup of rice, but the flour was tracked with paw prints and mouse droppings. The sight of it turned my stomach. I still had some salt, two pieces of jerked meat, and half a loaf of bread. With the lone squash left over from our garden, I figured I could make do until Rick came home.

I kept my meals small, eating only a few bites, chewing slowly and telling myself that I was full. Rick would be home soon. I had hope, until it started to snow. Now my brain was so clouded, I couldn't remember anything but snow.

Rick's new sweater was knitted and wrapped in brown paper with one of my old hair ribbons tied around it. It no longer gave me pleasure to imagine Rick opening his present on Christmas morning. Every good thought had been driven from my head by the sharp pains of relentless hunger, which had now dulled into a steady ache. Whenever I stood up, dizziness washed over me and my trembling legs seemed only just able to carry me from one place to another. Mostly I sat in the rocking chair, too weak to push the rockers into motion.

Between the giddy flurries of white, I could see that the snow was piling as high as the woodshed roof. Soon I'd have to go out and clear the narrow path. My foggy brain latched onto the thought that I wouldn't want to starve to death and freeze to death, too. I'd go out soon, after I rested.

Heavy pounding on my door yanked me from a dream filled with roast beef and boiled potatoes swimming in gravy. "Rick!" I called, my heart alive with hope. I struggled to my feet and stumbled to the door, fumbling with the latch before pulling it open. My heart about leaped out of my chest when I found myself face to face with an old Indian man. Intelligent black eyes looked out at me from the web of wrinkles that criss-crossed his face. Deep lines ran from either side of his nose to the corners of his mouth.

"Oh!" I gasped, a curious mixture of fear and relief chasing around in my head. Here was proof at last that I wasn't the only person left on earth. Yet should I be afraid? Why had he come? As if to answer my unspoken question, the Indian raised his arm. I flinched before I noticed the pair of rabbits dangling from the old brown hand. The Indian had brought me food.

Instantly, I opened the door wider. "Come in," I invited, moving my hand toward the middle of the cabin just in case he didn't understand English. He shook his head and held the rabbits out to me. I took them. He turned and walked away into the snow, a quiver of arrows hanging from his back and bow slung over his shoulder.

I didn't stay to watch him disappear into the storm. I was too busy stoking the fire in the stove and thinking of food.

After I had eaten both rabbits, I had enough strength to go outside and clear the woodshed path. I carried in two big armloads of wood and gratefully settled in for a sound night's sleep.

In the morning I woke to the familiar pangs of hunger, now sharpened with the recent reminder of food. *Why had I eaten both rabbits?* I berated myself. I could have saved one for breakfast. Tears of frustration burned my eyes. If only I could live like a bear and sleep until spring, it would solve everything. Maybe I'd just stay in bed anyway. There was no reason for me to get up. It would be so much easier just to lie here and sleep forever.

I wiped the tears out of my eyes and turned my head toward the window. I stared out the small pane of glass, not daring to believe what I saw. The snow had stopped. My heart lifted with hope, and I swung my feet out of bed. Sunlight was exploring an unbroken expanse of white. Now Rick would come home.

I boiled the rabbit bones and made a thin broth to drink before I busied myself straightening the house and stockpiling the firewood, trying my best to ignore the hunger that complained and rumbled around in my stomach.

As the weak winter sun began dropping in the sky, my spirits dropped, too. My repeated trips to the window to look for Rick were all wasted. I never spied him riding to my rescue along the snow-clogged trail.

The knock was startling and unexpected. I hurried to open the door and found the same old Indian who had been there the day before. I smiled and invited him in again. He didn't reply, but he held out a bird as big as a chicken. When I took it, he held out his other hand to me. His cupped palm was full of a tangle of brown shreds that looked like bark. I looked at him, puzzled. He swirled his fingers over the palm full of bark, then made his hand into a cup shape and pretended to drink from it.

"Oh! Tea!" I said, excited that we were communicating. The Indian nodded, and the corners of his mouth curved up. The lines from his mouth to his nose deepened even further, like two small canyons. I suddenly realized that this must be the Indian Rick had rescued. I smiled and nodded at the old man and held my hand out toward him. He dumped the bark into it, then turned and walked away.

I hurried inside and made my solitary meal. I carefully saved the soft under feathers that I plucked from the wild bird. If I could get enough by next Christmas, I would make Rick a new pillow.

The silent Indian continued to bring me food once a day. I invited him in each time, thinking that he might want to step inside and warm himself, but he never did.

One day I was raking ashes out of the stove, idly wondering what the old Indian would bring me for my supper, when I heard a shout. I hurried to the window and stared in amazement at a horse and rider plowing through chest-deep snow before I screamed, "Rick!"

I ran to the door and flung it open. "Asa!" Rick yelled. He slid off the horse's back and struggled through the snow toward me.

"Rick!" I called again. Tears spilled down my cheeks as Rick grabbed me into his arms so hard it hurt. I didn't complain. I was too busy crying into his coat.

When at last he pulled away, tears were running down his face and losing themselves in his beard. "Asa, I was so worried when I couldn't get back here, I thought . . ." He didn't finish. His face crumpled and he hugged me to him again.

"I wasn't sure you were coming back," I said through my tears.

"Oh, Asa, I'll always come back to you," Rick said. He pulled away and looked into my eyes. "I started back as soon as I could, but I got lost in the snow. Some of the Indians from the tribe I told you about last time found me and took me to their camp. They made me stay with them until it was safe to travel. It seemed like an eternity."

"Then they must have sent the old hunter," I said.

Rick tipped his head at me in confusion. "What old hunter?" he asked.

"You know. The one you found on your last trip that was too sick to move." Rick's eyes went wide. "The one with the wrinkles and the mouth lines as deep as canyons," I reminded him.

Rick closed his mouth and swallowed. "What about him?" he asked.

"He brought me food while you were gone," I said.

Rick looked around the snow filled landscape. "When did you see him last?" he asked.

"Just yesterday," I said, watching my husband's face warily. He was acting so strangely. "He brought me a leg of venison."

Rick began shaking his head in denial. "He couldn't have, Asa," he said.

"But he did!" I insisted.

Rick gripped my hands in his. "It couldn't have been him," Rick said searching my eyes with his. "He died the day after I left him with his people."

*Hal Jackson recounted this true story from an account he read about a young couple who was homesteading in the Teton mountain range in Idaho in the mid 1800s. On one of his forays into the mountains, the husband rescued an old, sick Indian man and returned him to his village. In spite of his efforts, the Indian died.*

*In winter the husband went to town for desperately needed supplies, leaving his wife at the cabin with enough provisions to last until his return. An unexpected blizzard clogged the trail and forced the man to delay his return home or die for sure. When he finally got through, he feared that his wife would be dead. He found her alive but weak. When she described an old Indian who had come to the cabin with wild game after her food ran out, it was the same man the husband had tried to help.*

# CEMETERY SHEEP

I trailed the sheep over the rise. I stopped dead when a cemetery dotted with wooden markers came into view. The sheep didn't notice my heart skip a beat. They kept their noses to the ground, following the sparse tufts of late summer grass that dotted the foothills.

The lonely graveyard was set a mile or so from town, a leper cast out of the city. A shiver darted down my spine, and I stood frowning at the grave markers that sat above the resting place of somebody's dearly departed. When I was alone, I wasn't ashamed to admit that I was shy of coffins and everything that went with them, and the blame rested squarely on the shoulders of my older brother Ted.

By the time I was seven years old, my parents had added so many kids to our family that they assigned Ted and me to a room in Grandpa's shop next door. It was nice to be away from all the crying babies in the night, but there was a problem. Grandpa was the undertaker.

In order to get to our bedroom, we had to walk past rows of caskets balanced on sawhorses in the upstairs workroom. It was especially hard for me to go to bed after dark, when the caskets crouched like hungry animals, watching and awaiting the day when they would swallow me whole and fill their empty wooden bellies.

At other times I just knew that there was somebody inside the coffins, trapped but not quite dead, because in the dark of night I could hear the caskets creaking as though a body was rolling over inside, trying to get more comfortable. Or trying to get out.

The only thing that made my new room bearable was having another flesh-and-blood person in it with me, even if it was only Ted. I didn't want to look like a sissy in his eyes, and I took comfort from his warm and living body breathing evenly in the dark, closer to me than the coffins that creaked in nightly complaint.

After we'd spent a couple of years in our new room, cousin Beth and her family came to visit. She sure looked different than the last time I'd seen her. She was still blonde and blue-eyed, but at thirteen, she had turned into the most beautiful girl I had ever seen. I envied Ted being closer to her age because the two of them spent a lot of time together. I tagged along, wondering why, oh why couldn't I have been born first?

I wanted desperately to show Beth the one and only thing that I liked about Grandpa's job. His hearse. It was polished white and parked in a garage that took up part of his ground floor shop. The hearse tongue always faced the wide double doors, ready to be hitched up to the team of horses that would pull it and its ghoulish burden to the cemetery.

I greatly admired that beautiful buggy, with its snowy fringe and gleaming white paint. The intricately carved detail around the top of the long buggy and around the driver's seat were fuel for my fancy, turning the hearse into stuff of high adventure. My imagination saw it as a royal coach, or sometimes a rescue vehicle for rich people in danger who were always happy to reward me handsomely for saving them. It seemed such a waste to use this splendid vehicle to carry dead people to their final destination. They didn't even appreciate the ride.

I imagined asking Beth to take a make believe ride as I pretended to be a Musketeer rescuing the beautiful princess, but I was afraid she'd laugh and tell Ted, so my courage failed me.

One evening I was sitting on the back steps of the house carefully carving a piece of willow into a whistle. If it turned out perfectly, I would give it to Beth as something to remember me by.

The sound of hurried footsteps broke my concentration. It was Ted, his eyes wide with worry. "Hoyt, you've gotta come," he said.

"What's the matter?" I asked, rising.

"It's Beth," Ted said. "You've gotta come see."

Troubled by the intensity of his voice, I followed my brother toward the hearse garage. The sun was nearly touching the western horizon, signaling the time that I usually headed for the bedroom in order to avoid the cold gooseflesh that always rose on my arms when I had to pass the creaking coffins in the dying light. No time to worry about that now. Beth needed me.

I followed Ted into the dusky garage. "Where is she?" I asked. Ted headed for the back of the hearse. "Is she hurt?"

"Worse than that," Ted intoned somberly. A warning chill prickled the hair at the back of my neck.

Ted opened the back doors of the hearse and climbed inside. My feet didn't want to move. I thought longingly of the warm kitchen and the chatter of my mother and Aunt Sophronia as they cleaned up the dishes and talked about baby colic and the new dress that the next-door neighbor had worn to church last week.

Ted stuck his head out of the back of the hearse. The last ray of the failing sun slanted through a small window in the wall and touched Ted's face, bouncing an eerie, unnatural gleam off his eyes. Then the sun buried itself behind the mountains. For the unnerving expanse of a split second, he hadn't even looked like my brother. "Are you coming?" he asked.

The impatience in his voice propelled me toward the yawning hearse doors. It wasn't so dark inside that I couldn't see the closed coffin that was kept in there as a display. Grandpa only pulled it out when he needed the hearse to carry an actual dead body.

I was alarmed to see Ted kneeling beside the polished wooden box, his hands resting on the edge of the lid, his thumbs poised to lift. My heart caught in my chest and I wanted to tell him to stop, but my voice wouldn't work. Ted slowly lifted the lid.

I was absolutely horrified to see Beth's body lying still and white, her hands folded stiffly across her chest. I quit breathing. My heart broke, pushing a hot wave of tears against my eyes. It couldn't be, not Beth. How could she have died? She hadn't acted one bit sick at supper. She'd eaten everything on her plate. It didn't seem possible. Did Uncle Angus and Aunt Sophronia know? Who would tell them? Oh, Beth!

Ted began to laugh, a maniacal sound that made me nearly jump out of my skin. Then Beth's corpse moved, and I squealed in fear, backing out of the hearse doors. She sat up, her flour-coated hand pointing at me in derision as she joined Ted in hearty laughter. My thumping heart slowed and my face grew hot with anger and embarrassment. I rubbed the tears off my cheeks and sprinted for my upstairs room. I was too angry to notice if the coffins were creaking as I stormed past. I hoped that Beth and Ted were still down there, listening to my feet stomp good and hard across the floor. I hoped they were sorry they'd played a stupid prank on me.

I flung myself onto my bed, fuming. Gradually my anger slid into regret. Perhaps my retreat had been too hasty. Here I was, alone in the room, my mind filled with images of Beth's dead face.

Boy, oh, boy, if Ted would pull that kind of stupid, mean prank on me to try to impress Beth, then he might try to scare me even worse when he came up to bed. I determined to stay awake and defend myself, yet in spite of my resolve, I was asleep before Ted came skulking up to bed.

Funny thing is, Beth never looked so pretty to me after that day. That was the pivotal point that filled me with a childish but very real aversion to coffins and cemeteries.

I pulled my gaze away from the old wooden markers and my old memories. I noticed that most of the sheep were lowering themselves to the ground. Oh, great. Normally I would welcome a chance to sit down and rest, but not beside a graveyard. Maybe I should just shoo them further along their way, but my employer, Mr. Jensen might see it as harassing his sheep and I didn't think he'd like it if he found out.

I threw another uneasy glance at the grave markers. They must have been set there fifty or more years ago when the earliest pioneers had buried their dead. Next to the cemetery was a skunk bush sumac colored deep red from the frosty nights just past. A cool puff of air scattered the crimson leaves across the old carved markers like a spatter of blood from a wound. I shivered. The cold air carried the promise of winter and the cemetery reminded me of my own mortality.

I checked the sheep once more. They were settled in little hillocks all across the field, rock solid in their repose. I finally resigned myself to my fate and sat down with my back against the flat side of a boulder. Stored heat from the sun radiated through my shirt and gradually relaxed my muscles. The sheep dogs took their cue from me and lay on the ground, their tongues out and their heads up as they watched the sheep. With the dogs so intent on our woolly charges, my eyelids grew heavy, and I fell asleep.

An angry voice startled me awake. Mr. Jensen was standing over me, his face red with fury. He flung his arm out. I stared in the direction he pointed, horrified to see several dirty white sheep wandering among the headstones, vagrant ghosts picking at the grass growing up between the grave markers.

"Get them out of there!" Mr. Jensen bellowed.

I jumped to my feet and whistled to the dogs. My heart thudded in my chest. Mr. Jensen didn't know that I'd rather die than set foot in a cemetery. "Petey! Shep! Captain! Go!" I yelled, pointing at the unsuspecting sheep. The dogs jumped up and raced for the errant animals, barking a warning as they streaked away. The dogs circled, their bellies close to the ground, striking at the slower sheep with quick nips. The sheep jumped and ran in panicked circles, kicking their feet in a vain attempt to avoid the dogs. They crowded together, frantic to get to safety in the center of the flock, crashing haphazardly through the grave markers.

I watched in horror as the carved wooden memorials of the dearly departed flew through the air and crash-landed onto the autumn-cold ground. The dogs were making things worse, not better. I'd have to tempt fate and go in there myself.

"Git going!" Mr. Jensen bellowed. "You lead them out of

there, and I'll set the markers to rights." He headed toward the graveyard, and then whipped around to glare at me. "Are you daft? Wake up, man! Head them off!"

My feet finally connected to my brain, and I headed for the irreverent string of sheep scattering in front of the eager dogs, hurrying to leave the scene of the crime now that the damage was done. Mr. Jensen stepped among the scattered grave markers and looked around, scratching his head under his hat. Then he bent and picked up one of the markers. He fitted it into the ground before he leaned on it, pushing down with all his weight.

I worked the dogs, bunching the sheep together as Mr. Jensen continued his daunting task. I suspected that he didn't really know where all the markers belonged, but he went doggedly about his work, as I did mine. I wondered if anyone who might come to visit this lonely cemetery would really mind laying flowers on the wrong grave.

*One of C. Hoyt Anderson's childhood memories stems from around the 1920's when his brother Ted took him to their grandfather, Andreas "Steamboat" Olsen's white hearse one evening to see what had happened to their visiting cousin, Beth. Ted lifted the lid of the plush-lined display casket inside, and there was Beth, pale and still. Hoyt's heart skipped a beat before Ted began laughing and Beth came "back to life."*

*Hoyt also recalls childhood memories from the age of seven or eight when he and Ted began sleeping in a summer bedroom at the front of Grandpa's woodworking shop. They could only reach it by walking past rows of caskets. Although the brothers used that bedroom for ten years, Hoyt admits that he never became comfortable walking past those coffins at bedtime, especially because they creaked in the still of the night (Saga of the Sanpitch, Vol. 27 pg. 19).*

*Lois Brown spoke to an unnamed sheepherder who confessed that his afternoon nap while herding sheep in the early 1900s near a small cemetery wreaked havoc when the wandering sheep ran from the sheepdogs he sent to chase them out of the graveyard, kicking the markers loose. The sheep's owner, also unnamed, replaced the markers in the dents in the earth, but seriously doubted that they were all put back where they belonged* (Saga of the Sanpitch, *Vol. 10, pg. 4).*

# A ROOM OF HIS OWN

The trip from the farm into town on the back of the over-loaded wagon, filled with all our earthly possessions, seemed to take forever. It didn't help that my sisters were chattering the whole way.

We finally groaned to a stop in front of a two-story house. I stood up on top of an old dresser, wondering if the odd little windows set in the roof looked out from my room. The half-circle shaped panes of glass were like none I'd ever seen before. They reminded me of eyes staring down at me from under curved eyebrows. A cold feeling of unease crept down my neck, and I shivered.

"Orion, what's the matter?" my little sister Jennie asked me.

"Nothing," I said. I squared my shoulders and tossed my head. Houses didn't stare at people. That was stupid. I was twelve years old, the only man in the family now that Pa was on the road with his new job. Men didn't get spooked.

I jumped down from the wagon and ran to the front door. I twisted the knob, disappointed to find it locked. A flash of impatience sent me trotting back to the wagon. As I held my hand out to help my mother down from her seat, my oldest sister Elna pinned me with narrowed eyes.

"Ma, would you like me to unlock the door for you?" I asked sweetly.

Ma's eyes got all soft and tender as she gazed at me. That was a good sign. I grinned at Ma, not bothering to hide my excitement. Ma fished around in her bag while Elna continued glaring at me. Soon Ma pulled out a large key and pressed it into my hand. The dull gray metal looked like pure gold in my eyes.

I dashed back up the walk, ignoring seventeen-year-old Elna's protests. "But Mama! Orion has to help us unload the wagon!" I knew Ma would let me find the room she'd promised

129

that I could have all for myself, up in the attic and far away from all my noisy sisters, before she asked for my help.

I fitted the key into the lock and twisted. The doorknob turned in my hand, and I stepped inside. The stairs yawned open across the hardwood foyer. A chill draft from the stairway twined cold fingers around my neck, arresting my progress. I shivered in my spot just inside the doorway and stared at the dim upstairs hall.

The very ordinary sound of footsteps on the walk behind me broke my trance. I hurried toward the steps, a sheepish smile on my face as I reminded myself sternly that of course it was cold. After all, this was March, and no fires had been lit in this empty house for a long time.

I wanted to be the very first to set foot in my new room, so I vaulted up the stairs by twos. I hurried along the second floor hallway past the doors that led to the rooms my sisters would share. One was for Elna and fifteen-year-old Lois. The other would be for nine-year-old Eloise and seven-year-old Jennie. The baby, another girl of course, was still little enough to sleep in my parent's room.

The door at the end of the hall led to the coveted attic. Elna had kicked up a fuss, protesting that it was horribly unfair that I got a room to myself because she was the oldest and should be the first to have her own room. Ma had said, "Now, Elna, be reasonable. Orion is twelve. He can't keep sharing with Eloise and Jennie." Elna had snorted, a most unladylike noise, the scowl on her face unmoved by Ma's explanation.

Ma sighed. "If it means that much to you, then I'll see if I can get a screen to put up between yours and Lois's beds. Then it will be almost like your own room."

Elna had thrown her hands up in exasperation. "You don't understand," she cried before sweeping out of the room. Well, too bad for Elna. Since my parents hadn't seen fit to give me a brother, the least I could get for having to live with a bunch of girls was a place I could retreat to when the giggling or quarreling got too much for me.

I flung open the door at the end of the hall and stared up at the attic ceiling. The sun lit up a small curtain of cobwebs hanging crookedly from the rafters. I would soon set that to rights. The spiders would have to move out, because I was moving in. I climbed the stairs and walked around the railing that kept the stairwell opening from being a dangerous drop. The center of my new domain was steep and high. The sides lowered themselves down to where I would have to stoop to reach the end walls. There was plenty of space for one—a spot for a bed, a wardrobe, and a nightstand. I could picture it all in my mind, and it looked mighty good.

As I turned back toward the stairs to get my things, a cold gust of air brushed the back of my neck. I shivered. Maybe Ma would make some curtains for those strange little windows after she got the rest of the house organized. I could wait, because I had my very own room to wait in.

I was disappointed when Ma said that we couldn't move my furniture up to the attic until Pa got home. She said that the stairs were too steep to tackle moving something as large as a bed without his help. "When'll he be back?" I asked.

"Maybe tomorrow," Ma said.

"You don't know?" I whined.

Ma turned to face me, and with uncharacteristic firmness said, "If you asked me when he was coming in from milking, I could tell you, but we don't live on the farm anymore, and your father's not farming, so we'll all have to learn to adapt."

"Sorry, Ma," I said. I guessed that she missed Pa, too. "Could I sleep in the attic anyway? I'll sleep on the floor." I could see Ma wavering. "I'll sweep it really good first, and I'll use old blankets. Please, Ma."

I knew I'd won the battle when I saw Ma's face soften into a smile.

"Thanks, Ma," I yelled, giving her a hug.

"Not so noisy in the house," she said with mock severity, raising her index finger.

I rushed into the kitchen and snapped up the broom, then

hurried upstairs to my haven. I began sweeping the dirt from the floor toward the staircase, kicking up big clouds of dust with the kind of energy that comes from intense pride of ownership. I turned toward the wall and bent over to push the broom clear under the steep slope of roof when I suddenly felt someone watching me. It must be Elna, coming up to inspect the prize that couldn't be hers. I felt kind of sorry for her, but there was no way I was going to give it up.

I pretended I didn't know she was there. After a minute or two, when she didn't speak, I decided that I'd point out how dirty the room was, and wasn't she glad she didn't have to clean up this dusty, spidery place? When I turned around, Elna was gone. I shrugged it off and went back to work.

That night, I snuggled down in my blankets on the floor of my very own room. It was hard to go to sleep, because I kept gazing at the walls lit with silvery light from the moon. At last I drifted off into a deep, contented slumber.

I woke when the moon had risen past the windows, leaving my attic murky and chilled. The steady tread of someone's quiet feet mounting the stairs reached my ears. I turned my head and stared hard at the railings. Would Elna be so mean as to get up in the dark of night and sneak up to my room? And for what? Maybe she was trying to scare me. Well, I could turn that game around on her.

I quickly lay my head back down and closed my eyes to slits, keeping my face turned toward the stairwell. The footsteps drew nearer. If only I could make her think I was asleep, then I could jump up and scare her good! She'd learn better than to invade my private space.

The footsteps continued, far longer than the staircase was long. What kind of tomfoolery was this? At the very least, I should be seeing Elna's head and shoulders by now.

Then the feet stopped. It was completely and eerily silent. There was no sound of feet headed up or down the stairs, not even on tiptoe. I couldn't see Elna, or anyone else for that matter. I opened my eyes wide. No one was there. My heart skipped a beat. I knew I was awake. The attic was empty. What was going on?

A chill breath of air blew across my head as soft and light as spiderwebs. I shivered, suddenly feeling very alone. I pulled the blanket over my head and waited anxiously for daylight.

By morning, I was over my childish bout of nighttime fear. I practically forgot all about it when Pa came home. In short order, we had my furniture moved up into the attic.

"Well, son, I like your quarters," Pa said. I looked around. Quarters. I liked that. Much more manly than "bedroom." It was good to have Pa home, especially since Elna didn't try any more of her sneaky tricks while he was there.

Pa helped arrange the rest of the household the way Ma wanted it. The piano was the hardest thing to move, but we finally managed to set it up in the parlor. I wasn't surprised when Elna was the first one to sit down and play it. She was such a showoff.

Each day was warmer as spring unfolded outside the new house, but the attic stayed cold. When I mentioned it to Ma one morning at breakfast, Elna looked smug. "That won't be a problem when summer comes," she said. "You'll be roasting like a little pig up there under the rafters."

"Elna!" Ma reprimanded, then she turned to me. "Son, why don't you keep the door open at the foot of the stairs? Maybe the heat will rise up to your bedroom and make you more comfortable."

I tried her suggestion that very night. Yet as I snuggled into my bed and pulled the comforter over me, the soft, steady footsteps started on the stairs again. In frustration I leaped from my bed and rushed to the railing. "Elna!" I called in accusation. My head cleared the railing, and the footsteps stopped abruptly. The stairs were empty. A prickle of fear crawled up my neck. Elna couldn't possibly have fled through the open door without me seeing her.

I backed up until my mattress hit my legs. I sank down onto the tangle of blankets. Never taking my eyes off the staircase,

I stuck my legs under the covers and pulled the blankets up to my chin with tight fists.

For the next couple of nights, I waited downstairs as long as I could before going up to my attic room. I didn't want to tell anyone that I was afraid. Ma would probably say that the house settling could sound like footsteps. The cold could be explained because it was April, a stormy and unpredictable month. So I kept my mouth shut and spent as little time as possible in the attic.

On the third night that I dawdled downstairs, Ma put her hands on her hips. "Orion, I've told you three times to go to bed," she said. "Now scoot!"

I lowered the book I was reading and stood up. "Good night, Ma," I said sadly, then dragged my feet toward the stairs. When I noticed Elna staring at me with a triumphant look on her face, I picked up my chin and marched up the steps.

I dove for my bed, then cringed under the covers, trying to close my ears to all sounds. After what seemed a long time, I fell into a fitful sleep that lasted until the wee hours of morning.

A rustling sound carried over from my dream. I awoke suddenly, instantly tense and listening, my eyes peeled open to an early gray light seeping in through the strange eyebrow windows. The unnerving titter came again. It sounded for all the world like the dry, whispery chuckle of shriveled leaves scattering across the street ahead of a dying autumn wind. Cold fear shot through me as the eerie laugh washed over me again in a frightening wave, pushing up gooseflesh along my arms and forcing my hair to stand on end. Then I heard the footsteps.

I pushed down into the mattress in a futile attempt to escape, horror paralyzing my limbs rigid so that I couldn't make them cover my head with the quilt, even though I desperately wanted to shield myself from whatever terror was mounting the stairs. When a white shape rose up above the top step, I forgot how to breathe. Fear crawled down my neck. The white thing moved toward me. My limbs trembled, and I was helpless to stop them. I wanted to scream but my throat wouldn't work.

The shape skimmed lazily across the floor and past my bed, pulling with it the familiar chill that had touched me so often. The cold swept my face and coursed through my body, setting my limbs to shaking so hard that I broke loose from the bed. Without conscious thought, I leaped from the mattress and scrambled toward the stairs. The ghostly figure continued its spectral journey across the attic floor as my flesh and blood legs hurtled me down the stairs and into the kitchen.

My hands trembled so violently that it was hard to get enough sticks into the stove to make a fire. I don't know how I got it lit. Perhaps it was sheer desperation. At last the warm and friendly flames took hold. I left the stove door open and huddled in front of the warmth, staring into the dancing fire and trying to absorb heat into my chilled flesh.

I was feeding another stick of wood into the hungry tinderbox when I heard footsteps behind me. A shiver of dread shook me from top to bottom, nearly knocking me off the stool, but I refused to turn around. I gripped the stick of wood as though it were a weapon and leaned in toward the fire.

"Land sakes, it's warm in here," Ma exclaimed. I let go a little moan and my shoulders sagged in relief. "How long have you been sitting there, Orion?"

"I don't know," I admitted. I turned and faced my mother. "Ma, I'm moving back downstairs."

Ma's eyes went wide. "Move downstairs?" she asked, planting her hands on her hips. "Whatever for?"

I looked away from her stunned expression and into the warm, comforting flames before I could make myself say, "Because the attic's haunted."

"Haunted?" Ma asked, her voice full of disbelief. "What makes you think that?"

"I feel eyes watching me, but no one's there," I said. "The attic's always cold. I hear footsteps on the stairs when there's nobody on them."

"Now, Orion," Ma said.

"I heard laughing," I said, shivering at the memory of the dead, crackly laugh that had chilled my bones.

"It could be your sisters," Ma said. "You're just imagining things."

I whirled around in my chair and stared into Ma's eyes, willing her to believe me. "I saw it!" I said.

"Saw what?" Elna asked as she padded into the kitchen in her long nightgown.

Before I could tell Ma to keep it to herself, she answered, "Your brother thinks he saw a ghost."

Elna's eyebrows shot up and her eyes took me in like I was a sideshow oddity. "A ghost?" she echoed, her voice dripping with contempt.

"He wants to move downstairs," Ma said.

"Not into my room," Elna warned.

"No," Ma sighed. "If he's really so afraid to be alone, I suppose he can move in with Eloise and Jennie." Ma looked at me with enough pity to raise a wall of resentment in my heart. Why wouldn't she believe me? "Are you sure you want to do this?" she asked. "Maybe it was a bad dream."

"Bad dreams every night?" I shouted in frustration. "Isn't there something wrong with that?"

"Not if you're suffering from a guilty conscience," Elna said in a superior tone that sent my hackles up.

I flung my arms out toward her. "Have the attic!" I yelled. "It's yours! I give it to you here and now!"

Elna stepped back, her eyes wide. "Maybe I will," she said, her dominant attitude shaken by my vehemence.

"We'll need to wait for your father to get home and move the furniture downstairs," Ma said in the pinched voice that she used to broadcast her disapproval.

"That's okay," I answered quickly. "I'll sleep on the floor."

I would not go back into the attic for anything. After Eloise and Jennie heard Elna laughing at my "ghost," they didn't want to go up there, either, but I finally talked them into getting my clothes for me. I stood at the bottom of the staircase and watched them walk up, stumbling as they leaned close together. When they reached the top, they glanced from side to side and locked arms. The sound of their footsteps crossing the wooden floor shot a shiver down my backbone.

In a minute or two, my pants and shirts came sailing over the banister, landing on the stairs like broken pieces of men, flat and empty as though the life had been sucked out of them. The girls came giggling and clattering down the stairs, kicking my clothes ahead of them as they went. Eloise rubbed her arms with her hands. "It's awfully cold up there," she announced. Jennie giggled nervously as I bent to retrieve my limp pile of clothing.

Pa had a serious talk with me about ghosts and imagination running wild before he moved my bed and wardrobe back down-stairs. I heard him grumble to Ma before he left for work again, "If Elna's going to move up there, why didn't we just leave them there for her?"

"She hasn't decided yet," Ma answered.

Pa shook his head. "If she does, get some of the neighbors to help you move her things. There are several young men in town who would be more than happy to show off their muscles to a young lady in distress."

Pa was on the road again when Grandma and Grandpa invited us to come over for supper. They only lived a couple of blocks away. Ma announced that we were going early so we could give them a hand.

"I'll be along later," Elna said to Ma.

"Are you trying to get out of chores?" Ma asked sternly.

"No, Mama, I need to practice piano," Elna answered, all innocence. "If I don't do it now, it will be too late by the time we get home." Ma looked unconvinced. "I'll clean up the dishes after we eat, Mama, I promise."

"All right," Ma said. "If it means that much to you, then you stay and practice, but don't be late for supper."

Elna broke into a grateful smile. "I won't!"

After our usual round of hugs, Grandma handed all of us blobs of her homemade wallpaper dough and pointed the way into one of the upstairs bedrooms. The dough was used to clean the wallpaper from the wood and coal soot that sifted through the house during the cold winter months.

As we filed into the room, I heard Ma say, "Mother, why are you spring cleaning so early?"

"I can't do it myself any more, so I thought I'd get a head start while I had all these busy little hands." Grandma smiled fondly over at us as we got busy with our blobs of doughy cleaner, rolling and dabbing at the walls. Grandma and Grandpa had pushed the furniture together into the middle of the room. We worked our way around the edges like newly captured horses exploring the fence line.

I was beside the window when I spied a most curious sight. Elna was running down the street as though her life depended on it, her skirt up around her knees, her feet pounding the ground faster than I'd ever seen them move before. I craned my neck to look beyond her to see what was making her run so hard. I expected to see a mad bull at the very least, but there was nothing.

I maneuvered around my sisters and the furniture to reach the doorway. As I hurried along the upstairs hall, I heard the front door click open, then bang shut.

"Land sakes!" Grandma exclaimed. "What on earth's gotten into you?"

"What's wrong, Elna?" Mama asked, alarmed.

Elna answered between great gasps for air, "That house is haunted, Mama!"

"What happened?"

"I was just playing the piano like I usually do, when all of a sudden it got cold. I pulled on my sweater and kept playing."

"Then what?" Ma asked.

"I was doing that difficult run along the keyboard when I suddenly knew that someone was watching me," Elna said. She glanced nervously over her shoulder at the front door. "I turned around to see if one of you had come home for something, but no one was there." Elna turned back to face Ma and Grandma. "I kept on playing, but something didn't feel right. I knew I wasn't alone." Elna shivered at the memory. "When I stopped playing to look again, I could hear someone breathing right beside me. But nobody was there." Elna took a deep, shuddering breath. "I ran. Just as I reached the door, I heard a strange noise, like a laugh mixed with leaves blowing across the ground." Elna grabbed our mother's arm. "I'm not ever stepping foot in that house again, Mama, no matter what!"

Ma pulled Elna into a hug. "It's all right, dear. You can stay at Grandma's house if you want to. I've been thinking that we ought to put that house up for sale."

Elna pulled back, her face puzzled. "You don't care that we just bought it?" she asked.

"So much the better," Ma said. "We don't have any attachment to it."

Elna cocked her head at Ma. "Mama, what have you seen?"

Ma stood silent, thinking. "Maybe a few unusual things that could be explained away, but now it doesn't matter," she finally answered. "You don't have any objections to selling it, do you?"

Elna shook her head. "No. The sooner the better." Then she looked past Ma and saw me standing on the stairs. She smiled an apology. "And when we find a new house, let's make sure it has a room for Orion, one that he can really call his own."

*In 1917, the Myrup family moved from the farm to a house in town where Orion, the only boy, would get the attic room as his own. His sister Jennie, who was seven at the time, recalls how Orion got ready for bed later and later each night until at last he declared that he was moving back downstairs because the attic was haunted. When teased, he declared that he had actually seen the ghost.*

*After he moved out of the attic, his oldest sister Elna, a mature seventeen, was home alone practicing piano when she felt a ghostly presence watching her. She flew out of the house to her grandmother's where her family was visiting, declaring that she wouldn't step foot in the haunted house again. Without admitting that she'd seen or felt the presence herself, mother Jennie put the house up for sale, even though her husband Niels was out of town on business. They moved to another house where Orion finally got his own room. This time he was able to keep it to himself* (Saga of the Sanpitch, Vol. 20, pg. 97).

# THE STRANGER

I had to set the full milk bucket down before I could open the cabin door. Mama's hair hung in wet strands around her forehead, and there were dark patches of sweat on the neckline and under the arms of her homemade dress. My baby sister Pearl was cradled in one arm. Mama awkwardly pulled open the oven door with her other hand. I breathed in the warm and wonderful smell of baking bread as I hauled the bucket inside, wondering if I should leave the cabin door open to let some of the hot out. "Adelaide, close the door," Mama said, batting at a fly with a dishtowel. I did as she asked.

"Take Pearl for me. There's a good girl." Mama smiled tired encouragement at me when I abandoned the bucket and opened my arms to take my three-month-old sister, who was dressed in a simple white gown and, for the moment, a dry diaper.

Mama turned back to the table, her hands moving quickly as she added ingredients to the large mixing bowl without measuring. "I've got to make another batch of bread or we won't have enough," she said. Pearl twisted up her face as though she might cry. "She just ate, so you need to hold her over your shoulder," Mama said as she began to stir the lumpy batter with a wooden spoon.

Obediently, I put Pearl up against my neck and patted her back. "How much bread do we need?" I asked. The food trunk in the corner of the kitchen had been steadily filling up with baked loaves for a the past two days.

"A trunkful," Mama said, her tired face cheerful as she measured salt into her palm and added it to the bowl. "It's a long trip to Salt Lake City, and I've figured out just what we need for the seven of us to eat each day. With the bread, dried pork and fresh milk from the cow, we should just be able to make it without going hungry." She poured milk into the bowl and again began stirring vigorously with the wooden spoon. "I hope there's enough flour," she worried aloud. She glanced at the limp flour sack sagging over the edge of the kitchen table.

"I wonder what Salt Lake City will be like?" I said as I wandered back and forth across the dirt floor with Pearl squirming on my shoulder.

"Oh, it will be wonderful," Mama answered, looking up at me with eyes as excited as a child's. She pushed up the sleeves of her dress. "We'll have a house with a real wooden floor, and we'll live close to my sister."

"Aunt Gussie?" I asked.

"Of course," Mama said. She plunged her hands into the mixing bowl. "She's the only sister I have."

"But won't that be confusing?" I asked, tilting my head to the side. "Even Granny said that sometimes she couldn't tell you two apart!" I knew I couldn't ever really mistake anyone else for Mama, even though she and Aunt Gussie were twins, but it was fun to see her face light up when I teased her.

Papa had just about all of our possessions loaded into the wagon. We would sleep in our old log house one more time, then in the morning we would head for Salt Lake City. I felt butterflies in my stomach at the thought. After living on this isolated flat near Ferron with no other houses in sight, I wondered what it would be like to have people living in a house right next door to me. I tried to imagine it, but I couldn't make it seem real, so I gave up.

The next morning, I awoke early. Mama was already up, placing the last of the bread she'd baked the day before into the food trunk. I climbed out of bed, jostling my twelve-year-old sister Amanda, who moaned. "Come on!" I said to her. "Get up! It's moving day!"

We had a simple breakfast of bread so fresh it was still soft inside. When I was done I hurried out and saw Papa leading our milk cow, Kickapoo, toward the wagon. When the horses, Ada and Stub, whinnied a greeting to their barn mate, Kickapoo looked at them with wide and curious eyes. Papa tied Kickapoo to the back of the wagon, saying, "You older girls will need to take turns walking beside the cow to make sure she's keeping up and not getting herself half-strangled in her rope." Papa gave Kickapoo a worried glance. "She's not used to walking very far."

"I'll do it!" I volunteered, my ten-year-old legs itching to hit the trail. I was ready to walk all the way to Salt Lake City. Besides, I'd rather walk beside the cow than stuff myself into the wagon alongside my three little sisters.

When we rolled away from our old homestead, my excitement grew. The further I walked, the more energy I had. I fairly skipped along beside Kickapoo, who was not moving fast enough for my liking. *I can walk faster than the cow*, I thought impatiently, *and she has twice as many legs*. I tried to enjoy the scenery, but the trees and rocks a couple of miles from home weren't any different from the trees and rocks next to our old cabin.

I glanced into the back of the wagon and noticed Amanda staring past me with watery eyes. I wondered if she'd gotten dust in them, but she wasn't blinking or rubbing them with her fists. I turned to see what she was looking at. All I could see was our plain old log house—square, brown, and unremarkable on the vast flat of land that we had lived on for most of my ten years of life. The barn squatted behind it, weather beaten and empty. They looked very small. I wondered if buildings had feelings. Did they know we were gone? Did they miss us? I felt a catch in my chest and resolutely turned my face forward. I avoided Amanda's sorrowful gaze and continued to tromp doggedly along beside Kickapoo.

When we stopped at mid-day to eat, the house was no longer in sight. I was grateful for the bread and pork that Mama passed around. It tasted wonderful and filled the hunger clawing at my belly. When lunch was over, Papa announced that it was Amanda's turn to walk with Kickapoo, so I crowded into the wagon, pulling my tired feet up close to my body. My little sisters dozed in the warm afternoon, and I found myself having a hard time keeping my eyes open, so I didn't try. I relaxed and slept.

The wagon braked to a stop, jolting me awake. I peeked out

the side of the wagon from underneath the cover. It was easy to lift the canvas in the sections where it wasn't tied down. A wall of rock blocked my view. The wagon cover strained against the ribs that supported it over our heads, puffing and snapping as it fought a stiff breeze. When I climbed down, a blast of wind hurrying down the canyon pushed me back against the wagon. I squinted my eyes against the swirling dust. I saw with delight that we had actually entered the canyon that would take us through the Emery Mountains and on to Salt Lake City. Papa had pulled off the dirt trail and stopped the wagon next to the wall of rock that had blocked my view. I couldn't tell how tall the mountains were from here, since their tops were buried in thick, gray clouds. A fresh gust of wind channeled down the canyon and swirled my skirt around my legs. It seemed to me an invitation to explore the road ahead, and I could hardly wait to get moving again.

My seven-year-old sister Lizzy climbed out of the tangle of blankets where she'd been sleeping, bent her head into the wind, and headed for the bushes, her mussy braids blowing out behind her. Mama hurried over to me and placed Pearl in my arms. "But, Mama," I began.

"Please, Addy, I need to get supper going," Mama said, flinging open the food trunk and holding the lid up against the wind. She seemed unusually agitated, and I decided it would be wiser not to protest any further.

I turned to Amanda, who had found some shelter from the wind beside the broad back of Kickapoo. "Will you hold Pearl?" I asked her.

"If you'll milk the cow," she answered.

"Half," I said.

"All right." Amanda took the baby from me, and I hurried to follow Lizzy into the undergrowth where I could heed nature's call with some modesty.

When I got back to the wagon, Papa was pointing up to the trail ahead of us and saying something to Mama. Mama bit her lip and avoided Papa's eyes. She wouldn't have been able to see him through her tears anyway. I hoped they weren't changing their minds about moving. I couldn't go back to the old homestead now. It would be like moving back into a cage.

"We've got to, Hanna!" Papa yelled at Ma above the roar of wind gusting down the canyon and shaking the trees until the leaves rattled. Mama didn't answer, but turned and walked to the back of the wagon where she began gathering up blankets.

"Addy, untie Kickapoo," Papa told me.

"What's wrong?" I asked.

"There's a storm coming. We need to take shelter," Papa answered. He worked at unhitching the team.

"The wagon's our shelter," I said, clasping my hands around my elbows when a sudden chill in the wind sent cold prickles up my arms.

Papa looked up at the sky roiling with dark gray clouds that blocked the sunset and smothered the mountains. Only an angry orange smear against the bottom of the clouds smothering the mountains proved that there had been a sun shining down on us this morning. "It looks like a bad storm," Papa said. "I found a cave that will hold all of us. We're going to stay there tonight." He grabbed both horse's reins in his fist. "Get the cow and follow me."

I hurried behind the wagon to untie Kickapoo. I walked between the rock wall and the wide-eyed cow, using her broad body as shelter against the increasing wind. The cave was just around the end of the rock wall, a surprisingly short distance from the wagon but invisible from where we had stopped. How had Papa found it at all? If we'd continued up the trail, we would never have seen it.

There was a wide overhang where Papa had sheltered the horses. As soon as Kickapoo caught sight of Ada and Stub, she began to trot. I had to run to keep up with her. She stopped beside the horses and they whinnied a greeting. The animals moved their feet restlessly.

Mama herded my little sisters into the cave. Amanda followed with the cooking utensils balanced in one arm and

Pearl held against her hip, the baby's little arms and head draped over the crook of Amanda's elbow. I hurried over to her and took Pearl.

"Thanks," Amanda said.

The cave was tall enough for Papa to stand in. The rough stone wall that curved around us was wider than our log cabin, but the dirt floor reminded me of home. Papa began to lay a fire and Mama said, "Amanda, Addy, you girls spread these blankets out over there." Mama pointed to one end of the cave. "Lizzy, help your sisters," she said. Then Mama rummaged in the food trunk.

A crack of thunder froze us in our tracks. It was startling the way the sound bounced off the rock and rolled around the cave, shaking me to my very bones. The thunder that crashed over our small cabin had always stayed outside, pounding on the logs but never getting through. After a second's worth of absolute silence, five-year-old Eva screamed. She buried her face in Mama's skirt and wailed. Lizzy looked startled, then her chin began trembling. Mama pulled her younger girls into the circle of her arms and soothed them with a quavering voice. "Hush. It's only thunder. We've had thunder before, it's just a big noise. You're all right." Mama's words and Pearl's soft, warm body held against my pounding heart helped calm my frightened breathing.

"Now, girls," Papa said. "Here's a fire for us. If you're cold, come sit by me. We're safe." He held out his arms to Lizzy and Eva. "Come let me hold you so Mama can get us some supper." The little girls scurried over to Papa, and a flash of lightning chased them the last few feet into his arms. I braced myself for another roll of thunder. It came on the heels of the lightning, cracking across the sky and rolling around the walls as it had before. I felt as though a huge, invisible boulder was rolling over me, squeezing out all my courage. What if lightning hit the cave? It could split the mountain apart and bury us underneath a mass of broken rocks.

I hurried over to Papa and the fire, leaving Amanda to

spread the blankets by herself. I reasoned that with Pearl in my arms, I wouldn't be much help anyway. I sat as close to Papa as my little sisters would let me and stared into the warm orange flames. Rain was punishing the ground outside the overhang. "Do you think it might have been like this with Noah in the ark?" Papa asked. "We could pretend that I'm Noah and you can all be one of the animals."

"I'm a kitty," Eva said, glancing up at Papa for approval.

Papa stroked her head. "Nice kitty, kitty, kitty," he said. Eva smiled with delight.

"I'm a horse," Lizzy decided.

Papa reached over and pulled up one of her braids. "What a fancy mane you have for a horse," he said. Lizzy giggled.

I couldn't understand how Papa could be so unconcerned about our perilous situation. How could he play at a time like this? If this really were a flood like Noah's, we'd be drowned! Caves didn't float!

The next lightning flash wasn't as brilliant as the first. I couldn't tell if it was because the fire lit up the corner of the cave where I huddled with my family, or whether it was because the storm was moving away. The thunder followed, sounding fainter than before, like the grumbling of a cranky old man.

Papa began telling the familiar story of Noah and the ark. Mama came over to us with a pan and fat piece of salt pork. Amanda was right behind her. Papa had set two flat rocks to one side of the fire. Now he used a stick to push some coals into the opening between the rocks. Mama set the pan on the rocks and put the meat in. Soon the smell of frying pork and the sound of Papa's deep rumbling voice made me feel secure and very hungry.

After Papa finished his story, he milked Kickapoo. The simple food was warm and satisfying, reminding me of suppers in our cabin. I felt a twinge of homesickness sitting in the cave, chilly drafts rolling across my back as the fire warmed my face. Shadows flickered on the walls behind the heads of my family like strangers trying to look over their shoulders. After family prayer, we rolled ourselves up in our blankets. I snuggled as close to Amanda as she'd let me before I could fall asleep.

We stayed in the cave for three days. The rain continued off and on and the clouds covered the sky with a solid lid of gray. More than once, I heard Mama ask Papa if we couldn't go on in spite of the rain. He always told her no.

The last night we stayed in the cave, Mama only took a piece of pork the size of her little finger and laid it on a half slice of bread for her supper. Papa didn't eat much, either. After we were tucked into our blankets, I noticed Mama bending over the food locker in the small circle of yellow lantern light, counting the loaves of bread, her forehead pulled down into a worried frown.

By the next morning, the clouds had cleared to the edges of the sky, leaving a broad expanse of blue in the middle. Mama stood next to Papa at the cave entrance. "The rain has stopped," she said. "Now can we go?"

Papa scanned the sky. "The trail will be slick," he said. "We need to wait until it dries out some." Mama threw up her hands in despair.

"It can't be helped, Hanna," Papa said. "It won't do us any good to get underway if we can't make any progress." Mama didn't answer him, but walked back to the blankets. She sat down and held Pearl in her arms, silently rocking back and forth, staring at the cave wall.

It was after our mid-day meal when Papa announced, "Time to go." He walked out to where Ada and Stub were grazing in the wet grass. He bent and removed their hobbles before leading them to the wagon. Kickapoo followed.

"Come on, girls, all of you help carry something," Mama said. She put a small stack of Pearl's clean diapers in Eva's arms. With Mama's urging, we soon had the wagon loaded and Kickapoo tied on the back. I volunteered to take the first turn to walk beside the cow. After three days, the refuge of the cave had become more like a prison. I began walking briskly, but before long, I regretted my hasty decision. In spite of waiting more than half the day for the road to dry out, there were places where the wet dirt stuck to my shoes, making a thick sole on each. They were heavy and became harder to lift the higher we climbed. Occasionally the mud sole became so heavy that it fell off. Then I had to walk with an awkward, uneven step. Yet as the afternoon wore on, the road dried out more, making it easier for the horses to pull the wagon through the steepening canyon.

Halfway through the afternoon, Papa stopped the horses. "Everyone needs to get out and walk," he said.

"Edmund?" Mama questioned, her eyes on Papa's face as she cradled Pearl close in her arms.

"The horses are working too hard," he said. "We all need to walk for awhile."

"It will take us longer to get there if the little girls have to walk," Mama said.

"We could stop and camp here for the night if you'd rather."

"No. We need to keep going," Mama said. Papa helped her down from the wagon seat, then stepped in front of the team. With reins in hand, he led them up the trail. Amanda took Lizzy's hand and I held onto Eva's. We followed Kickapoo, her hooves leaving deep prints in the damp, shaded places along the road.

After the steep climb leveled out, the trail curved around the side of the mountain for a ways. There was a meadow spread out like a green patchwork quilt on the down side. The other side was a rock mountain slope that slanted up and away from the trail. Flowers dotted the hillside with optimistic spots of color. "This might be a good place to camp for the night," Papa said.

"No, Edmund, let's go further," Mama said, glancing back at her daughters. "There isn't enough food. We need to travel as far and as fast as we can."

"All right, girls, the horses can pull you again for a while. Everybody in," Papa said.

I helped Eva into the wagon bed, and Amanda gave Lizzy a boost. She started to climb in after Lizzy, but I said, "Wait! I started out walking, so it's my turn to ride."

Amanda turned toward me, her face set in a scowl that made

me brace myself for an argument. Suddenly her eyes shifted beyond me. I turned to see what she was looking at.

An old man with a long white beard picked his way down the mountainside, skirting taller brush and rocks on his way toward us. When he got closer, I could see that his clothes looked as old as he was. His trouser hems were ragged, and his shirt was worn nearly through.

I glanced further up the slope to see if the stranger had a horse waiting for him. There were no animals or other people in sight. Who could he be? Maybe he was a sheepherder who had spotted our wagon. What did he want from us?

Papa stepped out to meet the stranger. The stranger smiled, weather-beaten crinkles beside his eyes radiating good humor. "Hello," the stranger greeted Papa. He pulled off his old sunbleached hat, stained with sweat. He nodded toward us girls as he twisted the hat in his hands. "Lovely family. How's your journey?"

"We were delayed by the rain," Papa said. "We're anxious to get moving again."

"Then I'll not keep you," the stranger said, turning his hat a little faster. "The fact is," he stopped speaking and glanced down at his tattered shoes, seeming reluctant to continue. Then he sighed deeply and glanced back up. "I'm very hungry and wondered if you could spare me some bread."

Papa spread his hands helplessly. "We haven't got much, and we've still got a long way to go and a lot of mouths to feed."

The stranger ducked his head apologetically, staring down at the hat as it passed through his hands, going round and round. Then he lifted the hat and placed it on his head. "I wish you Godspeed," he said, tipping the floppy brim. He nodded to the front of the wagon where Mama sat with Pearl on her lap. Then he turned and began his slow and tedious ascent. My heart was as heavy as his footsteps. Where was he going? What would he do? How could I eat my supper tonight knowing that he would be sitting somewhere, all alone and hungry?

"Wait," Papa called, turning and hurrying back to where I

stood with Amanda at the back of the wagon. He flung open the lid of the food locker and dipped his hand in. It came out with a whole loaf of bread. He let the lid slam down and strode over to the stranger. "Here," he said, holding out the loaf. "I hope it is enough."

The stranger took the bread in one gnarled hand, turning it over as though to make sure it was real. A smile lit up his face, and he swept his eyes around to each one of us before he nodded at Papa in gratitude. "Thank you," he said. "God bless you." Then he touched the brim of his hat and turned to climb up the mountainside.

I wondered what Mama was thinking as I watched the old man work his way up the slope, pausing often to negotiate the obstacles that got in his way. I hoped Mama wouldn't be angry with Papa.

Then something happened that made me forget all about what Mama might think. I stared in disbelief as the stranger faded. I groped for Amanda's hand, my eyes not leaving the figure of the man until he completely disappeared. The place he had been standing was unquestionably empty, and I hadn't even blinked. He was gone as though he'd never been there. The stranger and his loaf of bread had simply vanished.

I turned startled eyes to my sister, who moved her head at the same time to stare at me. "Did you see that?" I whispered.

"He disappeared," she answered.

Papa glanced over his shoulder at us, his mouth slack. He turned around to stare at the empty mountainside again.

"It was a messenger from God," Mama said, her face glowing. She made her way to the back of the wagon, Pearl clutching onto her shoulder with tiny fists, her head wobbling as she tried to look around Mama's neck to the hillside where the stranger had been.

I was shocked. If I hadn't seen the man vanish with my very own eyes, I would never have believed I'd seen an angel. Who would have thought an angel could look so scruffy?

I turned to Amanda. "I'll walk if you want me to," I said.

"No, you ride," Amanda said, her face gentle. "It's my turn to walk." I climbed into the wagon, and we continued our journey to Salt Lake City.

When we finally pulled up in front of Aunt Gussie's house several days later, Mama hurried in to greet her sister. Amanda helped Lizzy and Eva out of the wagon, I noticed the food trunk sitting in its customary place. Mama's prediction had not come true, because none of us had gone hungry.

My curiosity stirred, I lifted the lid and peeked inside. On the wooden bottom sat five whole loaves of bread. I softly closed the lid and jumped down from the wagon, eager to meet my cousins.

*Vida Sorensen of Spring City, Utah wrote down this true event that happened in the life of her aunt, Adelaide Sahlberg Thompson. Around 1902, the Sahlberg family was planning a move from Ferron to Salt Lake City where father Edmund had work. Mother Johannah began days ahead of the departure to make enough bread for the trip, carefully planning the exact number of loaves she would need to feed her family along the way. They set out with the cow tied to the back of the wagon, the older girls taking turns walking behind it to keep it moving.*

*A severe rainstorm caused the family to seek temporary shelter in a cave in the Emery Mountains, depleting their food stores. When they were able to resume their journey, the family noticed a bearded man in threadbare clothes approaching from the mountainside. Adelaide assumed he was a sheepherder, although she saw no sheep. The stranger asked for bread. Her father told him they didn't have much and were facing a long journey, yet after some thought, Edmund handed the old man a loaf.*

*The stranger gave his thanks, then the girls watched him head back up the mountain. The old man vanished, disappearing right before the eyes of the astonished sisters. Adelaide believed that the old man was sent from God. When the family reached Salt Lake City, they had an unexpected surplus of bread* (Saga of the Sanpitch, *Vol. 14, pg. 20).*

# FLUTE SONG

The haunting melody from an old Indian flute rose from the grooves of the aged vinyl Smithsonian record where it had been imprisoned more than sixty years before. The soul of the old love song was freed at last, note by heady note, as the record spun steadily on the turntable.

On impulse, Gary Fields pulled out his own homemade wooden flute. Fitting his fingers to the holes, he put the instrument to his mouth and blew a tentative note. Gradually the melody grew and ripened under his patient fingers. Finding his way along the path of the song maker, Gary followed the steps that finally ended in his own mastery of the deeply moving music.

Satisfied at last, Gary added the song to his repertoire of about fifty songs that he played in his Native American performances.

It was five years later when Gary found himself in Eagle Butte, South Dakota while traveling with a BYU performing group. He was visiting with Tommy Robideaux when Tommy suddenly said, "Hey, Gary, come with me."

"Where are you going?" Gary asked. He stood up and stretched.

"I want to introduce you to the Foolsbulls," Tommy said.

"The Foolsbulls? Who are they?" Gary asked, tucking his shirt into his waistband.

"Oh, you'll like them," Tommy assured him as he headed for the door. "You've got things in common."

"Like what?" asked Gary, his interest piqued. He followed Tommy out the door.

"Flutes," Tommy said, opening the driver's side of the truck and climbing inside.

Gary got in the passenger side. "Do they play?"

Tommy shrugged. "A little."

Gary leaned back against the seat and Tommy backed out of the driveway and headed out along the road. "What, they want lessons?" Gary prodded for information.

"No, nothing like that."

"Then what?" Gary asked.

"You'll see," Tommy answered, his eyes gleaming at his little subterfuge.

They soon pulled up to a modest house and Tommy jumped out. Gary followed at a slower pace. "Come on!" Tommy called, leaping up onto the porch. Gary let his gaze rove over the curtained windows and followed Tommy. He had no idea of what to expect.

A small, wrinkled woman answered Tommy's knock. "Tommy!" she cried, her wrinkles curving into a smile.

"I've brought you a flute player!" Tommy announced, pointing at Gary.

The woman's eyes sparked with interest as she took in Gary's features. "Well, well," she said. "A flute player. Come inside and let's see."

Gary followed Tommy into the dim interior of the house. The living room was a simple rectangle, unremarkable, except for what lay on the mantle. A very old flute rested on its side. Gary was drawn to it, the musician in him taking in the patient details of the old craftsman's art. He gazed at it while his mind wondered at the hands that had carved the instrument from wood darkened by years and worn smooth from repeated use.

"Go ahead. Pick it up," the woman said.

Gary didn't wait for a second invitation. He lifted the flute from the mantle and turned it over reverently in his hands, his curiosity teased as he wondered who had made the instrument and how old it was.

"Play me something," the woman suggested.

Gary shot her a startled look. "Well, I don't know," he hedged. "Every flute is made differently, and you can't play just any song on every flute. They usually don't sound the same." Gary looked down and twisted the old flute slowly around in his hands. "I'm not used to this one, and I don't know if my songs will sound very good."

"You certainly won't know if you don't try," the woman replied. "You and I both know you want to. I can see it in your eyes."

Gary certainly did want to try out the old flute, but he would rather do it alone for the first time than in front of this audience of two. Yet the flute was warm and inviting in his hands, feeling very at home there, and he couldn't see how he'd ever get another chance. Besides, an off note or two with a couple of extra listening ears wouldn't make or break his career.

He lifted the flute to his mouth, wondering which song he should play. As soon as the worn mouthpiece touched his lips, the old love song from the Smithsonian record sprang into his mind. It flowed down through his shoulders, traveled his arms and poured into his fingers, moving them along the path of the melody as they danced over the holes.

The flute was true, the notes sweet, the instrument effortlessly pulling the music from Gary and sending chills along his arms, pushing the hair on the back of his neck up to stand on end. He had never played like this before. He was caught up in something bigger than himself. He was no longer merely a man playing an old flute, but felt himself as one with something bigger, surrounded by the invisible life force that music claims as its own, as real as life that emanates from the soul of a person or animal. A spectrum of emotion raced through Gary's heart as his fingers found their flawless way over the unfamiliar territory of the old flute. Yet oddly enough, it didn't feel like a stranger. It was inexplicably right, a natural home for Gary's hands although they'd never visited there before.

Gary was carried along in the wondrous emotion that defied words. When at last he hit the final note of the song, the flute lingered on his lips for a moment before he finally lowered it with bittersweet finality.

Total silence greeted him. Tommy and the woman sat speechless for several long moments before Tommy's voice came out in a hushed whisper. "Where did you learn that song?"

Gary was puzzled at Tommy's intensity. "I just heard it on an old record a few years ago and taught it to myself," Gary explained.

Tommy shot the old woman a sideways look. Her unblinking eyes were staring straight at Gary, but her eyes weren't focused on him. They were fixed steadfastly on the old flute.

Tommy turned back to Gary. "That flute was made by Tom Foolsbull," Tommy explained. "He died ten years ago at the age of ninety-five."

"Oh, I'm sorry," Gary said, unsure what this bit of information had to do with him. "A relative?" he asked, tentatively, wondering at the woman's fixed gaze. The woman nodded, but didn't speak. A single tear spilled out of her eye and found its way down her cheek.

Tommy stared into Gary's eyes, "I haven't heard that song since before Tom died." Tommy's gaze shifted to the flute, and Gary looked down at the old piece of wood clutched in his fingers, every eye in the room momentarily captured by the instrument. "Tom made that flute to court the young woman who eventually became his wife," Tommy said. "You just played the very first song that Tom made on that flute, and you played it exactly the way Tom did."

*In 1980, Gary Fields, descendent of the Lakota and Cree tribes, found an old Smithsonian archive record titled "Folkways" a project to preserve Indian songs. Originally recorded around 1911 by Francis Denzmore on an old Edison wax cylinder, Gary found himself entranced by a particular love song. He taught himself the melody on his homemade flute.*

*Five years later, Gary traveled to Eagle Butte, South Dakota with a BYU performing group. While there, Tommy Robideaux took him along to visit a family that had a very old Indian flute. When Gary was invited to play it, the only song that came to mind was the old love song. As he played, he realized that something big was happening. In his own words,*

"That song came out of the flute itself. The hair on the back of my neck stood up and I got chills."

When the last note died away, the spirit connection was verified. The flute in Gary's hands was Tom Foolsbull's, who had made the instrument as well as the very song that Gary had just played in order to court his wife nearly 100 years earlier. Tom Foolsbull died in 1975 at the age of 95, so the flute was most likely made before the turn of the century.

Indians don't write songs, they make them from a bigger presence, a spiritual something that is all around us.

# DADDY'S GIRL

"Mama, Sena's too hot," I said. I picked my baby sister up and looked into her little pink face. I peeled back her blanket even though it was December and the snow was piled up in little white hillocks outside.

"Give her to me," Mama said, wiping her hands quickly on her apron before reaching out for my three-month-old sister. She lowered her mouth to Sena's forehead, checking the baby's temperature with a gentle kiss. She lifted her face and said, "You're right," just as Ellery coughed hoarsely from the bed he shared with Emmanual. Both of them were feverish and weak. Only Orrin was well enough to be up and doing a few chores.

My eyebrows raised with worry. "Do you think she's got the pneumonia?" I asked.

Ma's mouth sagged, and I thought she might cry. "I'm afraid so," she answered.

The dreaded epidemic had run its way through town, causing at least as many deaths as the Indians had during the old Walker War. The hearse had been making regular trips to the cemetery about a mile north of town, parking between the freshly turned graves as it unloaded another coffin into its final resting place.

I had been counting us as one of the fortunate families, since no one in our household had made that trip in the hearse to the cemetery. I figured it was because Papa was on a mission to Iowa, doing his best to teach the gospel to people who needed it and didn't even know it. I figured this must be one of the blessings we got for doing without our Pa.

I felt terribly sorry for Sena when she fussed and moaned in her cradle, not understanding why she was so miserable. Still, everyone else had pulled through, and with Papa still on his mission, there was no reason to think that Sena wouldn't be blessed to fight her way through this bout of fever as well.

A week or two later, when Ellery was finally getting up and around, Sena was much worse. She lost interest in eating, suckling for only a few seconds before falling asleep in Mama's arms, her breathing noisy as it fought past the congestion, her head lolling heavily in the crook of Mama's elbow. Sena slept nearly all of the time. None of Mama's remedies made Sena any better. When the baby did wake up, her eyes would stare out at nothing. She never smiled anymore. I missed seeing her cheeks pulled up in chubby delight when I cooed at her. It seemed that all her energy was being used up just to breathe.

Mama's eyes were shaded with dark circles. I tended Sena whenever I could, but her struggles to breathe made me feel so helpless, that I would often leave the room. Watching Mama try to do everything made me feel guilty, so I'd sit with the baby again, my heart breaking for my tiny little sister.

At last Sena was delivered from her suffering. Her spirit left her fevered little body and she lay limp in Mama's arms. I started to cry. "Geneva," Mama said, putting one arm around me, her voice thick with tears. "Look at Sena's face," she whispered.

It took me a moment to wipe the tears out of my eyes so I could look down at the baby. Sena's pink cheeks were smooth and plump. Her long lashes rested on the top of her cheeks like two little butterflies. Her labored breathing was stilled, replaced by an awful silence that left her brow smooth and unworried. Her face wore a look of utter peace and contentment.

"See?" Mama said, her voice breaking with tears she fought to hold back. "Our baby is with God now, and she isn't suffering anymore." Sena's body began shaking, and I gasped. My heart beat wildly as I wondered for a second if she were coming back to life, getting ready to cough her airway clear and stay with us for a while longer. Then I realized it was Mama's sobs that were making Sena's body move. "She was too good for this world," Mama said, her voice so full of anguish that I could barely understand what she was saying.

Mama wrapped Sena in her shawl and made her mournful

way to the undertaker's. When she came back, her arms were empty. My heart mirrored the aching emptiness as I watched Mama sit in the rocking chair and begin to rock back and forth, her arms curving automatically into a loving circle that would just fit a three-month-old baby inside.

I sat across from her and clasped my hands in my lap. Mama spoke without looking at me, her eyes staring straight ahead. "I asked Brother Wimmer to build the casket with a window," she said. I sat silently sharing my mother's misery. After a moment Mama spoke so softly I had to lean forward to hear, and even then I wasn't sure I heard her right. "I don't want her to be scared of the dark."

The funeral was cold and sad, just like my heart. I didn't want to watch them lower my baby sister into the dark hole in the ground that seemed to be as deep as the earth was wide. My head knew that Sena's spirit wasn't in that casket, but my heart didn't. Her dear little face showed plainly through the window, a little cherub who had flown to heaven, leaving just the shell behind. I memorized her beloved features, burning them into my memory so that I would never forget her.

When we got home, Mama put Sena's cradle in the shed and wrote to Papa to tell him that he wouldn't be meeting his baby girl when he returned. His letter a few weeks later read:

*Oh, my dearest, how my heart aches that you must go through this alone. My pain at the loss of our baby daughter has all but stopped me from living. This new little one, to be taken before I could even see her, even hold her in my arms once, seems a cruel punishment to bear. Yet I must trust that the Lord does what is right, as hard as it is for me to understand.*

*Please, tell me everything about our little Sena. Was she cheerful, or sober? Did she have a dimple? Was her face more closely resembling yours or mine? Please write all you can, and spare no detail. I had so looked forward to meeting this littlest girl of ours, and now she is gone. I am bereft. I pray for* strength, but my heart is weak. I pray you speed your response, as anything you can tell me about our baby would soothe my soul.

Tell the children I love them. Remind them that their Father in heaven loves them, and is holding their baby sister right now in his arms. Give them each a hug for me. This heavy loss has taught me that our children are precious gifts, and I cherish each one.

All my love in the gospel of Christ, Your ever loving Joseph.

It was not quite two years later when Papa made his joyous return. He told us that he'd stopped at the cemetery and visited Sena's grave on his way into town. He'd put summer wildflowers on the little mound of earth that covered her tiny body. His eyes were wet, and he hugged us each in turn with arms so tight they almost hurt. He had to be re-introduced to the boys, as he kept mixing them up, only able to keep their names straight if he saw them standing all together.

Papa got right back into community affairs as he had done before his mission. We were all extremely proud of him when he was elected to the city council. He was given charge of the cemetery. Permission was granted for him to secure a ten-acre piece of land just outside of city limits for a brand new burial ground. We eagerly joined him in planting trees and shrubs along the pathways laid out on the new piece of land. I helped Papa plant a wild rose bush along the fence line. He poured water onto the freshly tamped earth from the bucket he carried with him, then stepped back to survey our handiwork.

"I love roses, Papa," I said. "They smell so heavenly."

"Yes, Geneva," he agreed.

The new cemetery was receiving new residents regularly as the old pioneer cemetery was abandoned. People were very pleased with all the grass, flowers, and young trees, which made the new cemetery a beautiful place to visit. It was much easier to irrigate the new plot than the old one, which was so far out of town.

"Geneva," Papa said to me one summer morning. "I'd like you to come and help me today."

"All right, Papa," I said. I climbed into the buggy without question. I figured I'd find out where we were going when we got there.

When we headed north out of town, I could see the scattering of headstones in the old cemetery far ahead. My eyes always sought them out when I rode this way, drawn by the magnet of my baby sister's grave. Papa turned in at the cemetery gate, so I wasn't surprised when he made his way to Sena's burial plot. He stood looking down at it for a moment before he reached into the back of the buggy and pulled out a shovel. My mouth dropped open in surprise when Papa put the point of the shovel on top of Sena's resting place and stepped his foot on the back of the blade.

"What are you doing?" I asked, even though it was obvious. Papa put his full weight on the metal blade and it bit into the earth.

Papa tossed the shovel full of dirt aside before he answered. "I'm moving Sena to the new cemetery."

"Why?" I asked.

Papa tossed another scoop of dirt to the side. "I miss her," he said. "I want her closer to us."

I was amazed at the depth of feeling that Papa had for this little daughter that he'd never even seen. Wouldn't it be easier for him to just forget she'd ever been? The only proof he even had of her existence was the letter Mama sent to him when Sena was born.

I watched silently as Papa dug, wishing for the first time that Mama hadn't chosen a casket with a window. Sena had spent four years under the ground, and I wasn't anxious to see her face. How would Papa feel when he saw a tiny little skeleton head that had been his baby girl? What would he do?

After some time of watching Papa dig relentlessly down into Sena's grave, I shifted my feet and worried that Papa might break the coffin's window. As though he'd heard my thoughts,

Papa laid down his shovel and bent way down to reach into the hole he'd made. He cleared the dirt from around the sides of a rectangular box. Then he gripped the edges and heaved the little box free from the earth.

I turned my head away. I wanted to remember Sena as she'd been before, not as the decomposed skeleton she must be now.

"My, but you're a pretty girl," Papa said in a gentle voice, as though he were speaking to a child. Startled, I turned my head to stare at him. He glanced over at me, a silly grin on his face. "I think she looks like you," he said, tilting the lid of the tiny coffin my way before I even had time to think of averting my eyes.

Sena's little face showed through the glass that Papa had swiped clear of dirt with his coat sleeve. I couldn't look away. Sena's face was pink-cheeked and plump, with little butterfly lashes lying gently on her velvety soft skin. It wasn't possible. She looked exactly as she had the day she'd been lowered down into the cold, dark ground four years earlier. If she wasn't withered and skeletal, she should at least have shrunken cheeks by now, yet by some miracle, she didn't. Sena was a perfectly beautiful little baby who could have been simply sleeping.

Papa cuddled the casket in his arms as though it were a simple wrap to hold his daughter in. He gazed fondly on Sena's flawless round face, a tender smile playing on his mouth. "Your mother and I," he said without taking his eyes off my dead little sister, "we make beautiful babies together."

Papa walked away from the grave and carefully loaded the small casket into the back of the buggy. Then, with his oldest daughter on the seat beside him and his youngest daughter in the casket behind, he shook the reins over the horse's back and we headed for Sena's final resting place in the new cemetery, under the rose bush that Papa had planted for her.

*Martha Rae Olsen tells a story of the year 1898, when three month old Sena Iona Anderson died of pneumonia while her father, who had never seen her, was on a mission in Iowa. Sena's mother buried the baby in a tiny casket with a window.*

*Many people used glass window caskets at that time.*

*After Sena's father Joseph Emmanuel Anderson returned from his mission on August 7, 1900, he was appointed chairman of the cemetery committee in conjunction with his position of city councilman. In 1901, a ten-acre plot was bought close to the city limits for a new cemetery. After shrubs were planted and walkways made out, Joseph took his oldest daughter Geneva to the old cemetery about a mile north of the town of Ephraim where he dug up his infant daughter. According to Geneva, her father said that his heart wouldn't rest until he had seen this precious child. When the dirt was cleared away from the window, the baby's body was perfectly preserved, even though it had lain in the grave for four years. Joseph gazed lovingly on the face of his baby daughter through the casket window before he moved her to a grave in the new cemetery (Saga of the Sanpitch, Vol. 17 pg. 94).*

# INDEX OF NAMES

**Rocking**
Edmund Theodore Sahlberg
Johanna Sandstrom
Margaretta Persson
Amanda Hannah Sahlberg
Adelaide Hulda Sahlberg
Elizabeth Elin Sahlberg
Eva Ester Sahlberg

**Shadow of Death**
(Incident reported as true, names made up)

**The Follower**
Joseph Franklin Hansen
Henry Mahonri Hansen

**Two Tickets, Please**
(Used same names as in original account, but unable to verify accuracy.)

**Horse on a Hill**
Betsy Bradley
Hyrum Bradley

**Best Friends**
Christiana Larsen

**Horse Traders**
Loyal Graham
Miranda Brady

**Message from the Graveyard**
George Farnsworth
Daniel Hamner Wells
Moses Franklin Farnsworth

**Cold as Death**
Lloyd H. Parry

**The Hideout**
William "Doc" Draper
Parley Draper
Effie Draper
Fanny Draper
Joseph Draper
Wilmont Draper

**Nine Lives**
Eardley Burdett Madsen

**Visitors**
Peter Alstrom
Daniel Hamner Wells

**Go Home**
John Henry Owen Wilcox
Mary Young
Hazard Wilcox
Sarah Wilcox

**Keeping Cool**
Eunice McCurdy

**Voices**
Shirley Reynolds Burnside

## The Clarion Haunt
Aaron Binder
Morris Reid
Teresa Reid
Bonnie Reid

## One Good Turn
(Incident reported as true, names made up)

## Cemetery Sheep
Hans Christian Hansen
Annie Margaret Neilson
Andreas "Steamboat" Olsen
C. Hoyt Anderson
Ted Anderson

## A Room of His Own
Niels Christian Myrup
Jennie Linda Fjeldsted
Mary Elna Myrup
Lois Marjorie Myrup
Orion Fjeldsted Myrup
Eloise Fredericka Myrup
Jennie Lind Myrup

## The Stranger
Edmund Theodore Sahlberg
Johanna Sandstrom
Amanda Hanna Sahlberg
Adelaide Hulda Sahlberg
Elizabeth Elin Sahlberg
Eva Ester Sahlberg
Pearl Margarete Sahlberg

**Flute Song**
Gary Fields
Tommy Robideaux
Tom Foolsbull


**Daddy's Girl**
Joseph Emmanual Anderson
Diantha Christiana Thomson
Geneva Christiana Anderson
Orrin Anderson
Ellery Anderson
Emmanual Anderson
Olive Dorthea Anderson
Sena Iona Anderson
Joseph Andrew Frances

# About the Author

Shirley Anderson Bahlmann grew up in New Jersey, with a vivid memory of her older brother DellRay jumping out, yelling "boo!" and scaring her so badly that she cried real tears! To his credit, he was suitably sorry, and apologized profusely.

Even after she moved to Utah with her family of mother and father, eight children, two dogs and a guinea pig, she never liked watching scary movies. Manti High School showed "Tales From the Crypt" one Halloween, and whenever the music got a lot of ominous sounding bass notes in it, she'd hide her eyes!

Never seeking the scary at Snow College where she served as editor of the "Snowdrift" newspaper, Shirley nevertheless entertained a curiosity about the unseen world of spirits and wondered if there really was any truth in the stories about haunted houses.

She's now married to Robert Bahlmann, is the mother of six sons, two daughters-in-law (Welcome, Jamie!), and a grandson. She currently lives in an un-haunted pioneer house in rural Utah.

"Unseen Odds" joins the ongoing "Odds" series, preceded by "Against All Odds," "Isn't That Odd?" and "Even Love Is Odd." Shirley's next work is a volume of true stories detailing interactions between pioneers and Indians, titled "How Odd!"

Shirley also enjoys hearing from her readers. Please feel free to stop by her website: at **www.shirleybahlmann.com**.